The Power of an
ORANGE
Chair

ANECDOTES, STORIES & CELEBRATIONS
OF AN ISAIAH 58 CHURCH

Ken Burkey

Table of Contents

PROLOGUE

PROLOGUE

I'm a pastor and I struggle with religion. I struggle with my profession a lot because of damage done in the name of religion and Christianity. I know people get hurt by other religions, but I can only speak for Christianity and its mismanagement and the abuse I have seen.

In the name of God, horrific things have happened in our world - wars, political power plays, sex abuse and more. Organized religion has used God as a power tool to gain control and leverage for personal pleasures — taking advantage of a world that wants to think that God cares and spiritual leaders deserve trust.

I struggle as a "religious leader" because all political parties have their own versions of Christianity and use those views to leverage political power.

When it comes to love, war, forgiveness, judgment, sex, money, relationships, material wealth, power and the way we treat those less fortunate, we forget the most important question: What did Jesus do and teach about those topics?

Turning the other cheek, serving the poor, forgiving our enemy, fighting injustice and giving up our possessions are nice Sunday School teachings, but they do not translate into our comfortable American lifestyles.

What do you say to someone who was sexually abused by a religious leader, or who was shamed and made to feel "less than" while trying to find their way as an adolescent? What do you say to the young woman who had an abortion, only to be kicked out of her church? How do you love the family who was marginalized because they did not have the resources to give to their church?

"Organized religion" quickly—dangerously—becomes us vs. them. The righteous vs. the unrighteous. The saved vs. the unsaved. The good people vs. the bad people.

Jesus once said, "The truth will set you free." With that logic, is there much truth in the religion and Christianity we see in our churches—with such a desperate lack of freedom? Instead of freedom, we see shame, despair, hopelessness, hurt and pain.

I find myself wanting to listen carefully to understand, empathize and love rather than just wanting to be right. When I just want to be right, I no longer care about the person, their passions, hurts, dreams, or their questions.

It may surprise you that most days, I question my calling and I long to connect with those who have given up on religion. My heart aches for those who have been hurt and for them to understand a true connection with God so they feel known, loved and protected. I find myself living with a very disjointed mindset where I long for God—for His forgiveness and His presence—but I feel so unworthy and selfish. I feel like "God" has lost so much credibility at the hands of the pastoral and religious world.

Perhaps you're asking an obvious question. "Then why are you a pastor? Why don't you stop whining and go do something else?"

Well, I would love to. But there is one reason and one reason only why I can't quit. It's this scandalous thing called grace.

Grace rocked my world when I was in college. I grew up in a religious home hearing about grace, but never grasping the grand enormity of the gift. Growing up, the teaching of Jesus competed with other philosophies and thoughts of the world. So in college, I felt very judgmental and narrow minded being a student of Jesus. I had a faith crisis. A big crisis.

I didn't know what I believed. I felt guilty for questioning my own faith, but I felt very judgmental questioning other people's beliefs. I felt numb. I felt lost. Whether people admit it or not, we all want to believe in something. My soul was empty so I began to look at my life. I knew I was flawed. I knew my motives. I knew my heart. My emotions were all over the place. I felt alone. Then I discovered that everyone has the same questions and the same feelings.

In college I was an emotional mess, but I could still see that if religion is about being good enough, joining the right church or having the right code of conduct, I didn't want to be religious.

But the Scriptures teach that inside of us, we all have a God-shaped hole that only God can fill. Power, possessions, pleasure or relationships cannot fill that hole. And I had a huge hole. That's when I discovered this thing called grace.

Grace, simply put, is a free gift offered to us by God. He offers His grace, His forgiveness, His redemption, His strength, His wisdom to us through what His Son Jesus did by going to the cross, taking our sins, our mess ups, our hurts, our pains our shortcomings and putting them on Himself.

Grace is a scandalous thing because it has nothing to do with our goodness.

Grace is hard to grasp. It takes a lifetime and more to understand. But I can tell you this: It's the opposite of religion. It's the opposite of what most religions say Jesus was all about.

I am a hungry student of grace.

When I began to explore grace, it changed my world. It made me less religious and more graceful (except on the dance floor). Grace made me less critical of others and more committed to growing my heart. Grace made me less fearful and I now live with purpose. I became less exclusive and much more inclusive after realizing grace is for everyone. I discovered freedom.

Jesus said, "The truth will set you free." Jack Nicholson said, "You can't handle the truth." But I think Jack was wrong. I think we can handle it. It can be scary—counterintuitive—but it will set you free!

The truth of Jesus will bring healing to replace hurt, joy to redeem sadness, direction in the place of confusion, and strength to overcome weakness.

For those of you who are hurt, shamed, abused and manipulated in the name of God, I am so sorry! My heart breaks daily as I live in this paradox of being a pastor, yet see the hypocrisy in our religious world and even in my own heart. But don't run away from grace. Don't run away from the truth that can set you free.

I am a student and pursuer of grace. My life changed forever in college when I discovered that Jesus was about grace.

The rest of the world operates on karma. You get what you deserve. But Jesus came and offered us this amazing, wonderful gift called grace, where we get something better than what we deserve.

Since grace happened to me, I don't judge other's beliefs or religions; I just hope they someday discover grace, because Jesus cut through all religious ceremonies and traditions to get to the heart of the matter. We need grace.

He did the only thing that could be done to get grace. It was the crucifixion.

This book aims to bring credibility back to the church and to obey Jesus' call to share grace in tangible ways to our world.

Credibility comes from obeying Jesus' teaching to shelter the homeless, feed the hungry, clothe the naked, love the rejected, touch the untouchable, fight for the abused, and take care of the widow and orphan.

When the church begins to share God's grace in those tangible ways, credibility will come back to the church. This is my life mission and my life goal.

The Most Important Thing in the World

"It is hard to explain, but you know it when you see it.
It is meek, but you can't contain it
Hard to grasp, but you know when it's around.
It is hard to teach, but it can be found.

Exceedingly quiet, while deafening loud.
It is extraordinarily humble, yet aptly proud.
Thieves want to own it, but it cannot be stolen.
Many are for the strong, it is for the broken.

No one's ever dreamed it.
No one's ever owned it.
No one's ever bought it.
You just get it when you receive it.
No politics can claim it.
No business can sell it.

No celebrity can wear it.
The poor and outcast possess it.
It is private, yet transforms communities.
Largely diverse, yet brings unity.

It is unfair, yet purely just.
More powerful than our strongest lusts.
Often emulated, yet falling short.
Eye for an eye, it is Karma's retort

Always talked about, yet seldom shown.
It is something you must experience to be known.
It is not so much a destination, than an eternal trip
You can't get by trying, you just open the gift.

It is multi-faceted, never looking the same.
It is the one thing that will never change."

This poem is about grace. Grace is a scandalous thing. It will get you kicked out of your religion. It has gotten quite a few people killed. Yet, grace is the only hope for you, me and our world.

INTRODUCTION

Introduction

Several years ago I gave a message inspired by Pastor Bill Hybels, Senior Pastor at Willow Creek Community Church. For this message, I placed different chairs on the stage. I had a bucket seat from a car, a dining room chair, an office chair, a lazy-boy recliner, a bar stool and a beach chair. Finally, I included a chair from our church auditorium.

Side note: Our church is known as the orange chair church because we have the ugliest, brightest orange church chairs in America. We have learned to celebrate these ugly orange chairs because of the miracles and life changes that happen in them.

I covered the orange chair to disguise it and I walked down each row, talking about how each chair represents something that we believe will fulfill our lives. The dining room chair represented physical nourishment. The work chair represented riches. The seat from the car represented freedom and independence. The bar stool represented pleasure. The vacation chair represented peace and relaxation. When I got to the end of the row, I came to the orange chair that was covered by a black sheet and I announced, "Ladies and Gentlemen, this seat may be the most powerful and life-changing seat you may ever sit in."

When I lifted up the sheet and people saw our cherished, iconic ugly orange chair under a spotlight, the congregation broke into spontaneous applause. It was a moment of genuine celebration as many people realized where their lives would be had they never sat in one of those orange chairs.

Many marriages would remain broken. Addictions would still have control. Bitterness, anger and hopelessness would still rule, and a separation from God would still be a very likely reality. I closed the message with a Bill Hybels quote, "There is something supernatural that happens when the body of Christ comes together."

Yes, there is something that can only happen when the body of Christ comes together and remembers and celebrates God's promises and purposes for our lives. Through singing, preaching, and sharing our dreams with one another, our lives are richer and filled with hope. Hebrews 10:23 puts it this way, *"Let's see how inventive we can be in encouraging love and helping out, not avoiding worshiping together as some do but spurring each other on, especially as we see the big Day approaching."* (MSG)

James, the brother of Jesus said there is healing when we have people in our lives where we feel safe enough to confess our deepest fears and our wildest sins (see James 5). People must know that they are not alone. We must earn the right for them to open up and know they are around safe, caring people.

People in the church that only offer the 'right' answers are not effective at helping people find love. Churches must consist of loving, non-judging people who truly care about the lonely and hurting.

Years ago I asked our staff, elders and volunteer leaders, "What IS the Church?" Their responses inspired me. Their answers included:
A place to find grace
A community of people at all stages of their spiritual journey
A community of servants
A place of forgiveness
A place to build authentic relationships
A place of changed lives
A place to belong
It's where I finally found my real purpose
The bride of Christ
A place to heal
A place to hear God's truth
A light on a hill
Messy
Then I asked them, "What is the Church NOT?"
It is not religion
It is not a building
It is not a social club

It is not a place to get business connections
It is not a place to escape the world
It is not a place to judge the world
It is not a place to eat free donuts

What is the "Church"? Great question. There is not one verse in the New Testament that says, "They went to church." According to the Bible, it is actually impossible to "go to church."

If you have ever said, "I'm going to church today," you would actually be making a theologically incorrect statement. The truth is, the Church is not a building or a meeting. The Church is followers of Jesus who gather together with a sense of mission.

We can't go to church, because we are the Church.

When Jesus walked the earth, God served the world through Jesus. All God did, He accomplished through the body of Jesus Christ.

Today, God still works through the body of Christ. But the body of Christ is you and me. We are the body of Christ. We are His eyes, His hands and His feet.

The Greek word for church—ekklesia—from ek (out), and kaleo (call)—indicates that as a Christian community we are "called out" of our familiar places to unknown territories. God "calls us out" of our ordinary and proper places to the places where people hurt. He wants us to go where we can experience with them our common human brokenness and need for healing.

When we put ourselves in unfamiliar places with the poor, hungry and exploited, it changes us. We go to heal them, but in exchange God changes us forever.

I want this book to inspire pastors, Christian leaders and Christ followers to change their language from "I go to church," to "I am the Church."

When people "go to church," the Church is weak and irrelevant.

When people live out, "I am the Church," the Church becomes powerful and relevant. We can celebrate God's working through us to give hope, healing, purpose and life.

This book is not well-rounded. I am purposefully redundant in this book. This book is about what it looks like to be the body of Christ. I will share "orange chair" stories that inspired Green Valley Community Church to up our commitment to be a church that draws people to Christ. Our commitment is to not only talk the talk, but walk the walk.

The Green Valley Dream is a dream where those who are hurting, hopeless, discouraged, frustrated or confused can find love, acceptance, guidance, hope, encouragement
and forgiveness.

It is a dream of sharing the good news of Jesus Christ in our community and beyond to the world.

It is a dream of thousands of people growing together in spiritual maturity through learning together, serving together, loving together, laughing together and giving together.

It is a dream where our love for one another would attract people to Christ.

It is a dream where people will look at Green Valley and say, "Wow, Church is a good thing!"

It is a dream where every person uses their time, talents, passions and resources for God's purposes so that we honor God, by giving Him our all, by giving Him our best.

It is a dream where we continually reach back to invest in a new generation of children and youth who are our future leaders. It is where we look beneath the surface of their lives and see God's gifts and potential in them.

It is a dream where we will serve the poor, take care of the sick, and love those who have walked down the wrong paths of life because that is where you actually meet Christ.

It is a dream that we will keep simple. Love God. Love People. And we will allow no other issues to get in our way.

It is a dream where we will constantly put ourselves in situations where we can't do it ourselves. So that we will have to trust God and see Him do amazing things.

It is a dream to never play it safe, but actually believe that God came to seek and save the lost. And actually believe that God told us that we must lose our lives in order to save them.

IT IS A DREAM THAT GOD LOVES. It is a dream where He says, "You make yourself FULLY available to me.

Become fully available in your worship, talents, passions and resources. Be fully available to love one another, forgive one another and serve one another. Make yourself fully, wholly, unconditionally, unreservedly, unashamedly available to Me. And I will blow your socks off with the miracles that I want to do."

God says today, "Dreams do come true!"

Imagine this being the reputation and destiny of your leadership and church:

> *"You will be like a well-watered garden,*
> *like a spring whose waters never fail.*
> *Your people will rebuild the ancient ruins*
> *and will raise up the age-old foundations;*
> *you will be called Repairer of Broken Walls,*
> *Restorer of Streets with Dwellings."*
> **Isaiah 58:11, 12 (NIV)**

As pastors and church leaders, if someone promised us this reputation and legacy, I think we would sign up right now. We would do whatever it takes—re-prioritize, re-strategize— to make this happen.

Most pastors feel called into ministry to make a difference for broken, mistreated, lost souls.

Most pastors want to see their communities transformed to neighborhoods where love replaces hate, forgiveness replaces bitterness and dignity replaces judgment.

Most pastors want their churches to reflect the metaphors that Jesus used: light and salt.

Most pastors understand that the gates of hell will not prevail against the work Jesus wants to do. Most pastors know this, want this and pray for this. However, because of urgent demands from the already convinced (along with limited resources) it is easy to lose focus on the longstanding mandate from Scripture for the local church.

If you gave most pastors a truth-telling serum, they will admit that their souls are tired, their frustrations are high and they feel far away from the original reason they felt called to lead the church.

To be pastors and leaders who will leave a legacy as the re-builder of ancient ruins and broken walls, we must change. We cannot continue to do business as usual.

In the wise words of Albert Einstein, *"The definition of insanity is to keep doing the same thing over and over expecting a different outcome."*

But changes are happening.

Heroic pastors are making the change. They are seeing redemption of souls and restoration of cities. Pastors are living out the true fast of Isaiah 58, modeling the metaphor of Matthew 25 where Jesus says "when you have done it unto the least of them you have done it unto me." They are leading their churches in new and inventive ways to express love in their communities and they are experiencing blessings they never imagined.

These pastors find renewed vision and strength they thought they would never regain. They are finding that the difficulty of aligning themselves with the true fast of Isaiah 58 is a worthy fight. To change priorities and be a voice for the voiceless is worth it and they never want to go back.

When I examined what these Isaiah 58 churches, pastors and leaders had in common, seven attributes stood out. I prefer to call these common attributes, mandates.

A mandate is defined as "something that is given to you by your superior or maybe even a court official and it orders you to take specific action. If you do not follow a mandate, there are usually some repercussions."

Following these biblical mandates bring redemption, hope, generosity, freedom and glory to God. Not following these mandates makes the church benign, weak and unattractive, keeping people away from God.

"Conviction is worthless unless it is converted into commitment."
Thomas Carlyle - Scottish Philosopher, Historian & Writer

The seven mandates outlined in the following pages bring freedom because they can be applied to all different styles of pastors and churches, various racial, generational and economic demographics, as well as all denominations.

These seven mandates are not a new program or philosophy or fad. They are biblical. Anyone willing to live and offer grace to a broken world can use them.

These seven mandates create a strong, sustainable structure for God's Kingdom to come, for His will to be done on earth as it is in Heaven.

The Seven Mandates
1. **A deeply convicted, broken-hearted leader**
2. **A full expression of the redemptive "Gospel"**
3. **A culture of deep, consistent values**
4. **Long term vision informs short term strategies**
5. **Clear evidence of authentic transformation of volunteers**
6. **Measurable, effective "Isaiah 58" success in the church and community**
7. **A culture of celebration**

I would like to share our journey that we, at Green Valley Community Church, are taking to fulfill these mandates. With examples from our orange chairs, hopefully you'll find encouragement to help lead your church or ministry towards grace, the true fast of Isaiah 58 and walk away from the busyness and emptiness of religion.

These are the key passages that I will use throughout the book:

Isaiah 58:1-12 (NIV)
"Shout it aloud, do not hold back.
Raise your voice like a trumpet.
Declare to my people their rebellion
and to the descendants of Jacob their sins.
For day after day they seek me out;
they seem eager to know my ways,
as if they were a nation that does what is right
and has not forsaken the commands of its God.

They ask me for just decisions
and seem eager for God to come near them.
'Why have we fasted,' they say, 'and you have not seen it?
Why have we humbled ourselves, and you have not noticed?'
"Yet on the day of your fasting, you do as you please and
exploit all your workers.
Your fasting ends in quarreling and strife, and in striking
each other with wicked fists.
You cannot fast as you do today
and expect your voice to be heard on high.
Is this the kind of fast I have chosen,
only a day for people to humble themselves?
Is it only for bowing one's head like a reed
and for lying in sackcloth and ashes?
Is that what you call a fast,
a day acceptable to the Lord?
"Is not this the kind of fasting I have chosen:
to loose the chains of injustice
and untie the cords of the yoke,
to set the oppressed free
and break every yoke?
Is it not to share your food with the hungry
and to provide the poor wanderer with shelter—
when you see the naked, to clothe them,
and not to turn away from your own flesh and blood?
Then your light will break forth like the dawn,
and your healing will quickly appear;
then your righteousness will go before you,
and the glory of the Lord will be your rear guard.

Then you will call, and the Lord will answer;
you will cry for help, and he will say: Here am I.

If you do away with the yoke of oppression,
with the pointing finger and malicious talk,
and if you spend yourselves in behalf of the hungry
and satisfy the needs of the oppressed,
then your light will rise in the darkness,
and your night will become like the noonday.
The Lord will guide you always;
he will satisfy your needs in a sun-scorched land
and will strengthen your frame.
You will be like a well-watered garden,
like a spring whose waters never fail.
Your people will rebuild the ancient ruins
and will raise up the age-old foundations;
you will be called Repairer of Broken Walls,
Restorer of Streets with Dwellings."

Proverbs 31:8-9 (NLT)
"Speak up for those who cannot speak for themselves;
ensure justice for those being crushed.
Yes, speak up for the poor and helpless,
and see that they get justice."

Luke 4:18-19 (NKJV)
"The Spirit of the Lord is upon Me,
Because He has anointed Me
To preach the gospel to the poor;
He has sent Me to heal the brokenhearted,
To proclaim liberty to the captives
And recovery of sight to the blind,
To set at liberty those who are oppressed;
To proclaim the acceptable year of the Lord."

Matthew 25:31-40 (NLT)
"But when the Son of Man comes in his glory, and all the angels with him,
then he will sit upon his glorious throne. All the nations will be gathered
in his presence, and he will separate the people as a shepherd separates
the sheep from the goats. He will place the sheep at his right hand and the
goats at his left. "Then the King will say to those on his right, 'Come, you

who are blessed by my Father, inherit the Kingdom prepared for you from the creation of the world. For I was hungry, and you fed me. I was thirsty, and you gave me a drink. I was a stranger, and you invited me into your home. I was naked, and you gave me clothing. I was sick, and you cared for me. I was in prison, and you visited me.'

"Then these righteous ones will reply, 'Lord, when did we ever see you hungry and feed you? Or thirsty and give you something to drink? Or a stranger and show you hospitality? Or naked and give you clothing? When did we ever see you sick or in prison and visit you?'

"And the King will say, 'I tell you the truth, when you did it to one of the least of these my brothers and sisters, you were doing it to me!'

James 1:27 (NLT)
"Pure and genuine religion in the sight of God the Father means caring for orphans and widows in their distress and refusing to let the world corrupt you."

"There's a difference between interest and commitment. When you're interested in doing something, you do it only when it's convenient. When you're committed to something, you accept no excuses - only results."
Ken Blanchard –Author of the One Minute Manager

MANDATE 1

A Deeply Convicted Broken-Hearted
Leader

Mandate 1
A Deeply Convicted Broken-Hearted Leader

"A broken and a contrite heart, O God, you will not ignore."
Psalm 51:17 (LB)

"It is our wounds that create in us a desire to reach for miracles. The fulfillment of such miracles depends on whether we let our wounds pull us down or lift us up towards our dreams."
Jocelyn Soriano - Author, Mend My Broken Heart

Every leader and pastor who is living out the true fast of Isaiah 58 has a heart broken for the sick, the poor, the forgotten, the lost and the discarded. Leaders ready to reposition a church or organization toward fighting injustice lives in this broken-hearted understanding.

When Jesus saw harassed and helpless people, he referred to them as sheep without a shepherd. His heart broke and he responded in compassion.

If you examine leaders and pastors trying to lead their churches and organizations as ministries that heal, you find each of them share a defining moment of broken- heartedness. This moment was the point where they knew they could no longer do "business as usual".

A heart can't grow larger and more compassionate until it is stepped on and smashed to pieces.

In 1994, my first year as Senior Pastor at Green Valley Community Church, I took a team of 30 people to Mexico City for 8 days to work with impoverished children. We saw physical and spiritual poverty ravaging these young lives. This trip changed me forever.

In a city of 30 million people, the chaos, the poverty, the hurting, the disease envelops you. It was overwhelming to see the vast number of people struggling to survive.

We saw children who were poor but fed. Others were poor and not fed. None had material wealth. But I was struck by their bright smiles, the thankfulness in their voices and how happy they were in the simplicity of their lives.

We would tell them Jesus loved them and they would beam, "I know!"

With very, very little these kids celebrated life and God, expressing gratitude for everything around them. I envied their contented hearts. It made me see my own emptiness. Even with an abundance of material possessions and pleasures all around my life, they were much happier than me.

The clincher was when we had spent a whole day in the vast garbage dumps on the west side of the city. We drove for 40 minutes at about 20 mph deep into the heart of the dump. We arrived at this little town, built up out of the garbage and it felt like another planet. I thought of the old Mel Gibson movie, "Road Warrior."

The people were barely surviving. Many were dying of hunger as we tried to feed them. We had rice, beans and tortillas. I remember the starving little faces looking up to us, barely strong enough to receive the meal. Live electrical wires threatened our paths. Many of the kids were deformed from the lack of basic medical care. None of the kids knew about a world outside of the dump.

There was no hope. It was not fair.

Later that night in my hotel room, my emotions came spilling out uncontrollably. I cried. I yelled. I was weeping with sadness and yelling at God in anger! My emotions were a wreck. Many of us gathered together and just cried. What hope did those children have? Why was I so blessed? Why was I so discontent when I have so much? Why would God put those kids in that situation? Why doesn't God do something about it? Why doesn't somebody do something about it? I was a mess.

The next evening, we held a church service in a little church built on the outskirts of the dump. This local church reached out to people who lived there. I was in no mood to be joyful and optimistic. How do you speak about the hope of God in a dump like this?

During the music time, God spoke to me very clearly. I was looking around at the people attending the service. They literally lived in a dump. They were worshiping God, thanking Him for their blessings; smiling, hugging, and celebrating God's goodness.

I remember they sang in Spanish the words of the psalmist, "Give thanks to the Lord, for He is good, his love endures forever." I was in awe! The poorest people I had ever met were challenging my paradigm when it came to happiness and contentment.

These people lived gratitude and contentedness. It wasn't because of their material possessions or their career dreams. It came from something so much deeper. Something I needed desperately. They were living the words of Paul, "I have learned to be content in all circumstances."

They took an offering that night. For us. The rich Americans. I just began to weep! Our guide said, "We better take it or they will be insulted." So we did, I was so humbled while we hugged them and wished them well.

> *"When I hear somebody sigh, 'Life is hard,'*
> *I am always tempted to ask, 'Compared to what?'"*
> **Sydney J. Harris – American Journalist**

I went to Mexico City to help poor children, and what I discovered was rich children and my poor soul.

I learned two things. One, contentment only comes from knowing that we are God's children. Two, I am responsible to use the material blessings to help and serve those in need.

God clearly told me. "If you keep going down the path you are on—this obsession with safety and comfort and possessions—you will not finish the race I have for you. But remember this moment, so I can use your life to make a difference. Remember this moment because it will reshape your leadership and your church."

I would like to tell you that it reshaped my life, my leadership and my church instantly. But it didn't.

I got back home and the consumerist 90's church culture was in full bloom—building bigger buildings, expanding debt-filled budgets and spending the majority of our time figuring out the next big fad to grow our church and build our kingdom.

As a young, insecure pastor, overwhelmed with weekly demands, I foolishly focused on trying to keep everyone happy.

But that experience in the garbage dumps never left me. The smells, sounds and sight of starvation were seared into my brain. I can close my eyes at this moment and go back to those dusty, dirty, diseased filled wastelands.

My broken heart began to mess with my conscience. My church life was comfortable. People enjoyed the music and complimented the messages—measures of success in the 90's.

But there was a dissonance in my soul of what I knew needed to happen in the church and my broken heart for the vulnerable. All of a sudden, what I was doing seemed shallow and incomplete.

So at the turn of the millennium, I began to emphatically challenge my church and myself in more convicting ways for our church to lead by taking care of orphans, widows and outcasts.

Our core values began to change. Serving the poor became our number one value and the foundation we built everything else on. Previously, it was just one of many goals.

No matter how it happens, once a leader's heart breaks, it becomes difficult to do "business as usual".

It will be hard to play it safe.
It will be easy to be impatient to things that are not eternal.
It will be hard to people please.
It will be easy to say no to things that will distract.
It will be hard, but you will never want to go back to easy.

I wrote the following poem based on Psalm 68, where David says, God is a *"Father to the fatherless, defender of widows—this is God, whose dwelling is holy. God places the lonely in families."* (NLT)

This poem is dedicated to children all around the world that have been forgotten. It is for victims of injustice, war, disease, abuse, lust and greed. These are the children God asks the church to defend.

I wrote this poem thinking about the children of India, Africa, Mexico and our own inner cities. This poem shares a piece of each of them.

An Orphan's Voice

My mama's sick, my daddy's gone
My belly's empty, I'm all alone
I can't grow food, the ground is poison
Religion says, it's the path I have chosen

My papa lives in a new steel home
It's a solitary place, no room to roam
His hug feels good, I need to cleave
I have to go, and he can't leave

The man with car, driving up the street
He gives me things, always bitter sweet
I will find love, even if it hurts
Pain has become, the way I feel, the way I divert

He says he loves me, I want to believe
He beats me sick, my skin starts to bleed
My actions compromise, he's gonna make me rich
I need a new definition, love shouldn't feel like this

I sweat with fever, mosquitoes rage
Can't get a net, it's a two week wage
Rain forgotten, water brown
It's all I drink, intestines pound

Church round the corner says they have good news
But only open an hour a week, I am confused
They say that Jesus loves me, I better get in
I tell them, I need to experience God with bones and skin

Gunshots past my window, sunset brings a brand new show
I survive another corner, I survive another go
I'm told there is a God, I'm told he's a father
I've been burned before, I'm not gonna bother

New job in the city, there's a new hope pending
I've been lied to once again, now I'm a slave never ending
My parents think I'm safe, I'm making a living
I'm used everyday, more animal than human being

I have no value, I have no worth
Accidents happen, including my birth
I have no future, I have no sight
But I will survive today, I'm ready to fight

I need a dad, I need a mom
I need a house, I need a home
I'm one of millions, yet all alone
I'm looking for a place where love is shown

I've heard of children, with gold in their hand
I want to go there, this forgotten land
Where a bitter pill will make me better
Please someone notice, I'm praying for a letter

I want to go where children aren't fatherless
Where my bellies are full and the streets are harmless

I want to go where love doesn't hurt and mosquitoes don't kill
Where churches are trading and Grace is the deal

I want to go where I'm safe, no longer looking behind me
Where I can find God, my heavenly father,
who places the lonely in families

MANDATE 2

A Comprehensive Expression of the
Redemptive "Gospel"

Mandate 2
A Comprehensive Expression of the
Redemptive "Gospel"

"The Spirit of the Lord is upon Me, Because He has anointed me to preach the gospel to the poor; He has sent Me to heal the brokenhearted, to proclaim liberty to the captives and recovery of sight to the blind, to set at liberty those who are oppressed; to proclaim the acceptable year of the Lord."
Luke 4:18-19

"Christ will never be cool. Terrifying, life-changing, shocking, and iconoclastic, but never cool. Jesus is not me homeboy. The Gospel will always be "relevant" but never trendy."
Jon Foreman - Lead singer of Switchfoot

As God continued to convict my heart away from business as usual, I had to wrestle with how narrow the American church had become in defining the Gospel. Jesus' definition was so much broader.

Isaiah 58, Proverbs 31:8-9, Luke 4:18-19, Matthew 25 and James 1:27 (read these passages on page 18) helped me repeal some old theology prescribed for pastors to just get people saved, get them to Heaven and hang on until Jesus comes back - because there is no hope for this sorry, old world.

I grew up with this theology and it still guides much of the evangelical world. Sure, the church dabbles with charity. But we have not taken seriously enough the true kind of worship God explains in Isaiah 58. We forget that Jesus' prayed for His Kingdom to come, right now, on earth as it is in Heaven. We forget that he commissioned and enabled the church, the Body of Christ, you and me, to storm the gates of hell and rescue the poor, the blind, the lost, the addicted, the judged and the hungry.

Envision some kind of hell someone is living in, and Jesus has mandated and empowered us to go there and rescue them.

During Jesus' ministry here on earth, he looked at Peter and told him, *"I will put together my church, a church so expansive with energy that not even the gates of hell will be able to keep it out."* Matthew 16:18 (MSG)

In my opinion, Jesus never intended for the church to look like it does today. We have plenty of talk, a lot of meetings, discussion and debate, judging, hiding and inward focus. We spend resources on the "already convinced".

Most programs placate the converted. This programming leaves empty buildings and wasted space except for a few hours on Sundays.

Jesus always intended the church to lead in rescuing people from hopelessness, brokenness, darkness and despair. However, this is not for the faint of heart.

I respect the church I grew up in. It taught me that God loves me and sent His only Son to save me. I do appreciate their commitment to share that amazing truth with me.

But my church was benign. We sang songs, heard truths from the Bible, talked about how evil the world was and sent money to missionaries doing heroic things in very dark, desperate places. These missionaries were "storming the gates of hell."

While they were "storming," we learned to stay as far away from hell as possible in safety behind the walls of our church.

My church set up camp on a Christian cul-de-sac so that we were isolated and safe from all the evils of poverty and injustice and so we could help from a distance.

Once a year we would go on a church controlled, organized mission trip where we would do a "fly-by" of hell, quickly returning home to our safe cul-de-sac. We felt good about ourselves for going on the trip but quickly reverted back to safety zone and thinking that darkness was more powerful than light. We hunkered down and would wait for Jesus to return.

We missed so many opportunities to help people and missed so many miracles because our church was not willing to storm the gates of hell and rescue the hurting and the broken.

Sadly, the church I grew up in closed. Not because they were not good people, but because their mission was to play it safe. It was a mission to stay far away from where God was.

The power of God is waiting at the gates of hell. The power of God is waiting for men and women to proclaim, "We are the Church and we are expansive with so much energy that the gates of hell will not be able to keep it out." We need courageous men and women to tap into His power to overcome the significant needs of hurting people in this world living in poverty and oppression.

One of the turning points in the early 2000's at my church happened when I stood in front of my congregation and told them to "Go to hell!" After their initial shock, I told them that this was not my opinion, but it comes straight from the Holy Scriptures.

Basically, what Jesus was saying was that he was going to create the church to "Go to hell!" and rescue people from death. To me, that is good news!

Brennan Manning writes in his book The Relentless Tenderness of Christ, that "For many in the church, Christianity is not Good News. The Gospel is not glad tidings of freedom and salvation proclaimed by Christ but a rigid code of do's and don'ts, a tedious moralizing, a list of minimum requirements for avoiding the pains of hell."

Jesus invites us to come and join him on this amazing adventure where we storm the gates of hopelessness, loneliness, addictions, brokenness, injustice, prejudice, poverty and selfishness and we enter into the Kingdom of God, where His will is being done on earth as it is in Heaven.

Storming the gates of hell is not just for the radical Jesus followers who have sweet beards and wear open- toed sandals. Storming the gates of hell is what every one of us; every student of grace was created for. God calls every follower of Jesus to join the "storming."

The American Church has an epidemic of people who know a lot of rules but are they storming the gates of hell with Jesus? Now is the time. This is our legacy. This is not an obligation but an opportunity! This is not a burden but a blessing!

"Is not this the kind of fasting I have chosen:
to loose the chains of injustice."
Isaiah 58:6

During this formative time at Green Valley, we began to form a new language, some new phrases based on the teachings of the prophets and Jesus.

One of the phrases was, "We need to start moving from **charity** to **justice**." The comprehensive expression of the "redemptive" Gospel is not about charity but about justice.

Charity means to give to a person or an organization who will do the work of reaching down and lifting people up. They are what you would call a middleman, buffering you safely from the actual experience of reaching and lifting.

Charity allows you to help someone or a group of people without having to experience the pain or discomfort or inconvenience of what they are going through. Charity protects you.

But charity also robs you. It robs you of depth, purpose and the joy that can only come from reaching down and lifting up the people that your charity protects you from. Charity can distance you from God.

Don't get me wrong. We need charity. We need generosity. We need to give to causes that we cannot personally be involved with. We need organizations on the front lines of war, disease, hunger and extreme poverty. And they need our support. Yet ultimately, God is not a God of charity. He is a God of justice.

The Gospel is not about charity but about justice. Jesus took our sin so that we could be justified before God. And because God is a God of justice, we must be people of justice.

Justice is about a young girl in Africa being able to attend school because she doesn't have to walk 10 miles to get water each day.

Justice is about a mother in Guatemala having access to medical care for her children so they can live to age 5.

Justice is about an inner city student being given a quality education so they can dream, compete and have equal opportunities as adults.

Justice is about a foster child in America receiving a family support system to propel them toward a sustainable future.

Justice is about a hungry belly at the bottom of the caste system in India having the same access to food as the bulging bellies of the upper caste system.

> *"Where you live should not determine whether you live,*
> *or whether you die."*
> **Bono - Activist & Lead Singer Of U2**

Ultimately, justice is about people paralyzed by religion, hearing and receiving the good news of Grace!

Justice is harder than charity.
Justice demands results.
Justice requires skin in the game.
Justice means sometimes eliminating the middleman.
Justice means we have to get our hands dirty, our knees skinned, our egos humbled and our comfort shaken.
Justice means we must learn to get along with each other so we can accomplish a greater good.

Justice is harder than charity, but it is exactly in these hard places that we see and experience the heart of God.

Martin Luther King Jr. said, "Human progress is neither automatic nor inevitable... Every step toward the goal of justice requires sacrifice, suffering, and struggle; the tireless exertions and passionate concern of dedicated individuals." He also said, "Injustice anywhere is a threat to justice everywhere," which reminds us that we must be involved in local and global justice.

I am not sure if you will meet God in a worship service and I am not sure you will meet God in a sermon, but I am sure that you will meet God when you get involved in justice.

Pastors and leaders forget to celebrate the promises to churches involved in the comprehensive, redemptive gospel of justice. When Jesus says to feed, shelter, comfort, visit and clothe, he means "justice". It can be difficult but you will meet Him there through your actions and you will experience a joy that will not go away.

When the prophet Isaiah says to defend the defenseless and to fight corruption and abuse, he speaks of justice. Your legacy as a church leader will be as a rebuilder of walls and a restorer of cities. You will experience the sense of fulfillment you have been searching for.

When the writer of Proverbs says that when you give to the poor, you are lending to God and he will repay you well - you are doing justice. You may have to change your lifestyle, but you will learn to trust the God who will provide for your every need. His spirit of generosity will set you free.

The full, redemptive Gospel is about showing up. God asks us to show up for a grieving mother, a lonely elder, a sick child, a hungry family, a struggling addict, a lost soul.

As we show up knowing we can't solve every problem, God uses us as agents of healing and miracles happen. I see it all the time, by just showing up.

God has wired us all uniquely and impassioned us differently. Great things happen when each of us take ownership to use our talents and passions to fight injustice in our community and world. The Good News is attractive and God is glorified.

When we expand the Gospel beyond just getting people "saved" and we begin to live in God's Kingdom now, every talent, passion and experience is needed.

Another phrase that leads our church toward the comprehensive, redemptive Gospel is a statement by Craig Greenfield. Craig left a lucrative business career to care for orphans in Cambodia.

He said, *"You say you care for the poor. Tell me their names."*

We can no longer settle for charity, once we know the names and the stories of those living in injustice.

Justice is about meeting Jesus in disguise. Justice is about showing up.

Show up in your own backyard where orphans are called foster children. Show up to the jungles of Peru where mosquitoes kill children. Show up to the slums of India where young girls are violated. Show up to the famine deserts of Africa where bloated bellies scream for nourishment. Show up to the inner cities of America where young men are growing up fatherless and drug dealing is the career of choice. I challenge you to show up. Learn the names.

For big causes of justice and small causes of justice, let's start showing up!

Showing up looks like Harry Rehder who voluntarily leads our auto-ministry. He oversees dozens of volunteers who fix cars for single moms so they can get to work and have safe transportation for their children. Harry's team also works on cars for senior citizens so they can buy groceries rather than pay a mechanic.

Showing up looks like Ron Wells, a local auto sales owner who regularly gives cars away to single moms and to those trying to get back up on their feet.

Showing up looks like Marsha Rose, who volunteers weekly to create life-saving support for the mentally ill, forgotten and marginalized.

Showing up looks like Paul Geddes, passionate about farming, who volunteers to help plant and maintain a 20,000 square foot garden to supply fresh fruits and vegetables to the hungry.

Showing up looks like an 82 year old Berkeley graduate and civil engineer, Art Edwards, who is spending his twilight years running a nonprofit transitional homeless shelter. He helps people move from despair to dignity and hope and done so against all odds.

Showing up looks like a 10 year old girl, Claire Cockrell, who after seeing a film on the true fast of Isaiah 58 and learning how a $10 mosquito net prevents malaria, went to her local public school and raised $1,000 to purchase 100 nets and save hundreds of lives.

Showing up looks like retired firefighter Doug Shelstad who walks the halls of our local hospital, praying for the sick and introducing the dying to a Savior who offers eternal life.

I could go on with many more stories of these heroes. The point is that when people start expressing the Gospel through their passions and talents, they fight injustice at every level.

When you do it to the least of these, you have done it to me. When you do it to the least of these, you meet Jesus.

Have You Seen Him Lately?

When Jesus walked this earth he was seen by sinners, saints, rich, poor, insiders, outsiders, Jews, gentiles, believers and non-believers.

In John 1, John records, *"The Word (Jesus) became flesh and made his dwelling among us. We have seen his glory."*

The comprehensive expression of the redemptive "Gospel" was revealed when Jesus became flesh and made his dwelling among us.

And we have seen His glory.

I think of the woman at the well, the shame of five failed marriages and an outcast in her own village, soul parched and empty, going back to tell about this man she had met. She is transformed by Jesus' gentleness and grace, embraced by salvation's story and declares that His kindness is better than life. She sees the comprehensive expression of the redemptive Gospel in all its glory.

I think of the Prodigal son who was ashamed, hopeless and fearful. He is sitting at the banquet table set for his return, overwhelmed by his father's unreasonable mercy and renewed by his Abba's love. This rebellious but forgiven prodigal son sees the redemptive gospel in all its glory.

I think about Zacchaeus. He's insecure, empty, shallow, crooked and a betrayer of his own people. He slid down the lookout tree as fast as he could, generosity springing forth out of his bones transformed by God's patience. He goes home to have dinner with the Giver of undeserved gifts and this remorseful tax collector sees how comprehensive, expansive and glorious the redemptive Gospel is.

I think of the woman, ashamed of her past and tears in her eyes, anointing the feet of the One who did not judge her. And while the religious voyeurs are scoffing and condemning with hearts of stone, the Son of Man looks deep in her eyes. For the first time a man does not want to take from her. He wants to give her everlasting worth. She is restored by her Master's touch and this abused woman experiences forgiveness through the comprehensive, redemptive glorious Gospel.

I think of 10 untouchable men who are full of sores, being touched by Emmanuel, God with us. They are no longer exiled. He renews their futures and restores their dignity. Strangely, only one comes back to thank Him, and this grateful, healed man experiences the comprehensive, redemptive glory of the Gospel of Jesus.

Have you seen Jesus and his glory lately?

Today, we see Jesus dwelling among us and glimpses of his glory through the Church. Today we see the full expression of the "redemptive" Gospel at work where God's will is being done on earth as it is in heaven.

When a homeless man, broken by drugs and hopeless about the future, shows up to church on a Sunday morning and we love and shelter him, we see the "redemptive" Gospel at work. We see the hands and feet of Jesus, dwelling among us and in a tender, affecting way. We see His glory.

When a family, devastated from the loss of their teenage son, receives gentle love and deep care by a group of selfless volunteers on the funeral support and griefshare team, we see the "redemptive" Gospel at work. We see the hands and feet of Jesus dwelling among us, and in a heartbreaking, counterintuitive way, we see His glory.

When broken couples reunite, wandering students find direction, empty bellies get filled, tired hearts find renewal, restless souls find peace, over and over, we see the "redemptive" Gospel at work. We see His glory.

Have You Seen Him Lately?

MANDATE 3

A Culture of Deep, Consistent Values

Mandate 3
A Culture of Deep, Consistent Values

"The very essence of leadership is that you have to have vision. You can't blow an uncertain trumpet."
Garry Wills - Certain Trumpets, Pulitzer Prize Winner

"Successful, enduring organizations understand the fundamental reason they were founded and why they exist, and they stay true to that reason."
Patrick Lencioni -
Author, The Four Obsessions of an Extraordinary Executive

I became senior pastor at Green Valley Community Church in January 1994. I was 27. Looking back, I had no idea what a church could do in a community. I had no idea how much I could love the church.

I love Green Valley Community Church.

I love the seekers who walk through the door wondering, hoping that maybe God is the answer to their questions. I love the volunteers who selflessly love and serve our community using their time, talents and treasures to honor God. I love seeing people who were burned by religion set free by God's amazing grace. I love our staff. They serve tirelessly, with great passion and vision. I love our younger generation and our older generation. I love that we are a multi-generational church.

As a senior leader, I can choose to involve myself in many things in my church. But only a few things absolutely require my involvement. If I do not lead in these specific areas, then I will fail overall.

> **My number one responsibility as a senior leader is to make sure the vision and values of our organization are clear and supported by a sustainable structure.**

If I do this right, many other things will take care of themselves.

If I do this right, I must ruthlessly guard the vision and build a biblical structure to support the vision.

Let's start with the keeper of the vision:

To live out the Isaiah 58, Proverbs 31:8-9, Luke 4:18-19, Matthew 25:31-40, James 1:27 mandate, we must be the clear sounding trumpet of God's vision for the Church.

Our culture (including American church culture) can muddy God's vision for the church. Many of our styles and procedures contradict what Jesus had in mind when he told us to be witness to the comprehensive, redemptive Gospel in our own cities and around the world.

Here's the problem: Jesus exhorts us to worship in spirit and in truth, yet many churches miss the whole point.

The prophet Isaiah shows us the kind of worship God is looking for. Christians and churches have divided over styles and what kind of worship pleases God.

Most American Christians think of music and singing songs when they hear the term worship. When pastors and churchgoers answer the question "What style is your church's worship?" they really are asked, "Do you have loud guitars and banging drums and worship leaders with tight pants and tattoos? Or do you have organs and robed choirs using hymn books?"

God clearly show us his vision for the church and real worship when He spoke through the prophet Isaiah.

"Quit your worship charades. I can't stand your trivial religious games: Monthly conferences, weekly Sabbaths, special meetings— meetings, meetings, meetings—I can't stand one more! Meetings for this, meetings for that. I hate them! You've worn me out! I'm sick of your religion, religion, religion, while you go right on sinning. When you put on your next prayer- performance, I'll be looking the other way. No matter how long or loud or often you pray, I'll not be listening. And do you know why? Because you've been tearing people to pieces, and your hands are bloody. Go home and wash up. Clean up your act. Sweep your lives clean of your evil doings so I don't have to look at them any longer. Say no to wrong. Learn to do good. Work for justice. Help the down-and-out. Stand up for the homeless. Go to bat for the defenseless."
Isaiah 1:13-17 (MSG)

Real worship happens when our lives and churches reflect the work God calls for. This is the music God loves to listen to. This is true worship. Pastors and leaders must carry this message of true worship.

We must be courageous enough to refuse to be distracted by every complaint about music styles and remind people of God's definition of true worship. We know it is practically impossible to put a family of four in a car and try to agree with what music should play. As a pastor, do you really think you can get hundreds of people to agree?

People ask me "What style of worship do you have at Green Valley?" I tell them that our style of worship is to work for justice and be a voice for the voiceless. We shelter the homeless, feed the hungry, clothe the naked, fight for the defenseless, encourage the oppressed, father the fatherless and care for the widows."

As they look puzzled I say, "Oh, you mean what style of music do we have at our church?" And I tell them, "Well, we don't have robes or hymnals, but we do have loud guitars and banging drums and worship leaders with tight pants. But, we also have some pretty cool sounding keyboards and an inspiring choir." They either look at me like I have issues or they say, "Let's talk about that worship style again. I am intrigued."

When the church participates in "true worship, people find redemption and transformation. They find Jesus. When the church participates in "true worship" you experience stories like this:

A single mother with no religious background loses her son in a freak accident. She is alone, distraught and hopeless. We hold the funeral at Green Valley, and our funeral ministry team shows her love and compassion. She starts to come to church. She begins a long journey of learning about God's hope, strength, comfort and love. With no family support she comes to Mother's Day services alone. The emotions of a childless mother are overwhelming. But during the service, a pastoral partner named Rose sits beside her, never letting go of her hand. At the end of the service, Rose asks her if she has asked Jesus into her heart, and she has! A miracle! They exchange numbers; Rose is a saint and promises to call her to continue loving support. This hurting mother leaves church with a little more hope, a little more healing, a little less lonely...and eternal life!

This is the Church! This is "true worship!" This type of story reminds us of our vision to help heal broken hearts and set captives free.

Stories are important and powerful tools for a successful leader. We tell vision stories all the time at Green Valley. In large and small settings, we give the clear vision of the Church by telling stories.

In the words of Patrick Lencioni, "extraordinary executives create organizational clarity and then over-communicate organizational clarity."

In the words of Bill Hybels, "Vision leaks."

As senior leaders of our organizations, we not only clarify and keep the vision, but we share stories and celebrate the results of the vision.

Whether I am speaking or another teaching pastor is speaking at Green Valley, we always evaluate the message by asking, "Did he or she tie the vision of Green Valley to the message?"

Whatever the topic, there is always an example of God's comprehensive, redemptive gospel that we can and should share.

Stories of Isaiah 58 ministries and Matthew 25 lives are the most effective way of sounding a trumpet so that vision doesn't leak away.

I tell my staff that if someone comes to Green Valley for four weekends and does not fully understand our vision, we are not being effective stewards of God's mandate to storm the gates of hell.

Creating organizational clarity is the second key to successfully storming the gates of hell.

Successful senior leaders make sure the vision and values of the organization are reinforced by sustainable systems.

When I share with other church staffs what we do at GVCC, they commonly have a meltdown. I can see their initial excitement and then it dawns on them that this takes work. They are usually on the brink of burning out so increased work is not appealing.

They believe to accomplish this type of change, the same few, tired people will have to do more. That is when I have the staff and leaders read Exodus 18 where Moses' father-in-law, Jethro, warns Moses that he is on the road to burnout and that he is not an effective leader when he tries to take care of everyone's problems and needs.

So he gives Moses a very important teaching on what a biblical, sustainable structure looks like. He has Moses break everybody up into small, manageable teams.

After explaining this, I have the staff read Ephesians 4. Paul writes that God has given pastors and teachers and other leaders the job to equip the saints to do the work of the ministries.

We then review 1 Corinthians 12 to show again how every person, who has received salvation through grace, has the same Spirit but with different gifts. Every gift is important and needed to live out the call to love. I remind them that 'Super Pastors' do not exist. This term comes from the celebrity worship in our American culture.

I remind them that as senior leaders and pastors, our passions and gifts of leadership are deeply needed but they are not more important than the gifts of administration, helps, hospitality, intercession and shepherding.

I remind them that pastors have a huge role to play as broken-hearted leaders, but nothing will happen if we don't liberate, motivate and release the Body of Christ to be the hands and feet they were created to be.

We evaluate Green Valley staff like this:
"Does your vision line up with Isaiah 58,
Proverbs 31:8-9, Luke 4:18-19, Matthew 25, James 1:27?
Are you relentless with the vision?
Are you investing in volunteer leaders?
Are you building a sustainable, biblical structure,
based on Exodus 18, 1 Corinthians 12 and Ephesians 4,
much bigger than what you can do alone?"

This is a huge paradigm shift for most church staff. Most church staff think they get hired to get the job done. To do the work. While it is important for senior leaders to spend time in the trenches, our job and our mandate from God is to liberate the body of Christ.

This is the secret behind Green Valley.
I'm not great at shepherding.
I'm not great at administration.
I'm not great at hospitality.
I'm not great at counseling.
I'm not great at a lot of things.
I'm not a Super Pastor.

But we have a lot of people who are great at something. And if we can equip and release them to be great, then the Church will be great.

In my senior leadership role, God has asked me to be great at two things: First, keep His vision of the full, redemptive Gospel clear. Second, make sure we build a sustainable biblical structure where every Christ follower lives out the true fast of Isaiah 58 with unique passions and gifts.

Ginger Jacob is our Director of Community Care at Green Valley. She plays a strategic role in living out God's vision for the Church at Green Valley. Her journey to faith is inspiring. Her biblical structure for community care is right on point.

Ginger's story:
"I did not grow up learning to serve. I grew up chasing the American dream.

I'm from a middle class, hard working, two parent family. My parents owned and operated a small retail business for 35 years, a place where my sister and I worked while growing up and where we learned a strong work ethic. Something I am very thankful for today.

Both my mom and dad grew up serving in their churches. But early in my life they had a bad experience in church and walked away. I don't remember ever going to church beyond an occasional wedding or funeral.

Hard work, success, achievement: these were my gods.

All I needed to make me happy was attainable if I worked hard enough, went to the right schools, and landed the right job, house, car and husband. And so, that is how I lived my life for 40 years.

My first attempt at marriage failed miserably. But I pulled myself up by my bootstraps and kept moving forward.

I met Ron in 1985. We married in 1986 and had three children in five years. Unfortunately, I hadn't learned from my first marriage and soon we were going down the same path. We bought the right house in the right neighborhood, drove fancy cars and became members at the country club.

We struggled financially, but we clung to the idea that Ron just needed to work a little harder, earn a little more and we would stay ahead of the curve and our increasing debt. We would achieve happiness through these efforts.

Wrong.

In 1996, in attempt to correct our mistakes, we decided to move our family out of the Bay Area to slow our life down, get out of debt and start over. So we pulled up stakes, moved to Placerville and settled into a house we could afford.

Unfortunately, Ron still worked in the Bay Area, so every day he drove three hours each way for four years. He was stressed, exhausted and tense at home.

When I look back on those years it amazes me that we stayed together. Also, I am surprised we didn't seek help from anyone for our challenges. We just kept on moving forward doing the best we could.

Our daughter, Justine was seven when we moved to Placerville. The summer after we moved, a friend from Danville invited her to go to Mt. Hermon for Summer Camp. She returned to this camp the next two summers. Unbeknownst to us, she had been introduced to Christ and started praying for our family.

She began asking us to take her to church but we found a million reasons why we could not. We were too busy and didn't have the time. Dad needed to stay home on the weekend after driving all week, we had yard work, Little League and so on. The excuses were endless.

Our daughter remained persistent and one day she marched into my bedroom stating that she had found a church really close to where we lived. I started to think it might be a good idea to just go once so she would stop nagging us.

So we went. On Mother's Day 2000, our family walked into Green Val-

ley Community Church. I honestly was afraid of what might happen at a church service.

I remember as if it were yesterday where we sat, how the music made me feel, the practical message and how much I liked it. My spirits were lifted that day. I began to think for the first time in my life about something bigger than my will and desires. There was something here that I didn't have and I wanted to find out about it.

When we walked out the doors, Ron said to me, "I think we've found a church." With tears in my eyes, I agreed. In December of that year, sitting in an orange chair, I asked God into my heart. I remember saying to Him, "I'm not really sure what this means or what your plan is for me, but I know I need you, I can't do it on my own anymore."

That was the year 2000 and just the beginning of our journey. God has given us a purpose for our life. Our marriage is stronger. We have the tools we need to grow in Christ together. We have healthy, loving friendships and people who hold us accountable.

In 2006, 6 years into my journey with Jesus, I stepped into the role of Director of Community Care. God broke my heart for grieving families, under resourced seniors, single moms, the homeless and the hungry - all who we serve in Community Care.

God has shown me the joy that comes from serving which is why I am so incredibly passionate about creating opportunities for people to serve our community. I love to stand on the patio to greet volunteers as they return from serving in our local community through the Takin' it to the Streets ministry. They're exhausted but have huge grins on their faces. They tell heartfelt stories about the people—new friends—they served.

I honestly don't know where we would be if we hadn't walked through the doors of Green Valley so many years ago and said "Yes" to God. I'm thankful for His grace and forgiveness and for loving me through all my past, present and future mistakes.

Every day I read Matthew 6:33 "...and he will give you all you need from day to day if you live for him and make the Kingdom of God your primary concern." This is my life verse, my ongoing prayer and the way I choose to live the rest of my life."

Ginger's story not only reminds us of God's amazing grace and the huge potential of those sitting in our chairs (orange or otherwise). It also reminds us how important biblical structure is when it comes to building and growing God's Kingdom and healing our broken world.

Ginger is an extremely gifted leader when it comes to building sustainable, biblical structure. I often use her as an example of what a sustainable structure should look like in an Isaiah 58 Church.

Ginger oversees 3 paid staff people, but is also personally responsible for many major ministries led by volunteer leaders who coordinate hundreds of other volunteers.

Ginger oversees these important ministries, all run by volunteer leaders:

• The auto ministry that works on hundreds of cars a month. They also fix and give cars away to working single mom's and senior citizens. This is led by a full-time working engineer and a retired civil engineer.

• The Community Care booth, manned by dozens of volunteers for 5 services a week. People can come and learn how to get involved in serving our community and our world. A full-time working insurance agent runs
this one.

• The funeral support team represents hundreds of volunteers serving families during their most difficult time of life. Our church averages a funeral a week, mostly for un-churched families. A team of volunteer full-time workers and retirees are in charge here.

• The memory garden was built on our property so people can place the name of a loved one on a plaque on the memory wall at the entrance of a beautiful garden where people can sit, pray, mourn and remember. It is such a healing place. A couple started this ministry after their experience with the loss of a child.

• The 20 thousand square foot garden grows vast amounts of vegetables for us to give away to hungry people who cannot afford nutritious food. The garden team members all work full-time jobs.

• The grief share ministry offers a place to meet, share and heal after losing a loved one. This is available 52 weeks out of the year. A mother's support group, a suicide support group and a widow's support group have spun off from this. These volunteer team members also work full-time.

• The moving ministry provides physical strength and emotional support (and our community care truck!) on Saturday mornings to help seniors and single moms move. A full-time school teacher facilitates at least one move every week.

• The Stop-Trafficking ministry strategizes to eradicate this extreme injustice, both locally and globally. They raise awareness and money. They fill gift backpacks and collect gift cards for the local FBI to give to rescued girls. They help start rescue homes in our town and in the very difficult area of New Delhi, India. Full-time moms and business women lead this ministry.

• The Takin' It to the Streets projects happen on Saturday Mornings. Hundreds of volunteers go out into the community and build and repair wheel chair ramps for the elderly, fix roofs and decks, and serve the lonely and forgotten in very tangible ways - no strings attached. This is in the care of two single moms who work full time.

• The 1:27 ministry runs by the motto, "No Orphan Left Behind." This ministry educates and supports those who want to provide foster care or consider local and international adoption. Through classes and seminars, they teach families how to lift children out of poverty. An adoptive mother oversees this team.

These volunteer leaders also lead over a thousand volunteers. Ginger spends the majority of her time leading, supporting, encouraging and celebrating these volunteer leaders.

This is why Green Valley can do so much. Not because we can hire staff to solve every problem. At Green Valley, staff is very, very important and productive, but only when it is focused on doing the most important things: Clarifying vision and building sustainable structure.

We do so much not because we are so smart or that we have all the answers but because we are trying to live out biblical justice with biblical structure.

Becoming an Isaiah 58 Church will take courageous, focused, deeply convicted, humble senior leadership who will keep the vision clear and facilitate the building of a biblical, sustainable structure.

A Challenge To Spiritual Leaders

Distractions everywhere, doubters abound
Change the world? That reasoning is not sound
My face slaps reality, visions take back seat
My watch ticks fast, challenging great feats

I'm told be practical, I'm told to chill
I'm talked off my soapbox, told to stand still
Busy with mundane, busy with tasks
Children are dying, our backs to the facts

Conversing about the day, waiting for weekend
2 days to do nothing, yet many die before week's end
It seems strange to talk about my shallow fun
While food's missing in ground scorched by sun

Religion in the big lights, inaugurating the next star
How do we entertain them, we have to raise the bar
While churches woo the converted, the already convinced
There is a world giving up, believing God is "past tense"

We will win with arguments, we will win with laws
We will win with theology, we will win pointing flaws
Debating with bumper stickers, politicians bold and cunning
The TV preacher says we'll get rich if we give him money

We proclaim salvation, we say we believe
Then why do we pick sides, asking others to leave
Good overcomes evil, love wins over creeds
Our hearts need transforming, touching those who bleed

Grace is messy, we all need the same
Cathedrals too clean, finding others to blame
It's time to get dirty, it's time for heartbreak
No more empty words, and a faith that's fake

Time to serve the poor, it's God's investment plan
Time to open our doors to the homeless man
Time to live with less, so that children are blessed
Time to give our all, so that the world will know the rest

MANDATE 4

Long Term Vision Informs
Short Term Strategies

Mandate 4
Long Term Vision Informs Short Term Strategies

*"If you wait for perfect conditions,
you will never get anything done."*
Ecclesiastes 11:4 (TLB)

*"Waiting for clear confirmation that a decision is exactly right is a
recipe for mediocrity and almost a guarantee of eventual failure."*
Patrick Lencioni

*"Take time to deliberate, but when the time for
action comes, stop thinking and go in."*
Napoleon Bonaparte

Successful senior leaders sound certain trumpets of long-term vision and values that lead to strategies and events in the short-term. When your vision and values are deeply shared and ingrained in a sustainable structure, strategies will flow naturally and make sense.

You will be able to filter your strategies through the consistency of your vision and values, making program and activity decisions simple. You will also know how to scale your plans because you know how deep and wide your structure is.

Vision and values remain the same in the long term. Strategies come and go depending on the season, the passions and strengths of leaders and volunteers, and the local and global needs at the present time.

When strategies flow through vision and values, people hold lightly to programs. Your church will find it easier to let go of potential sacred cows. In fact, this will keep you from having too many sacred cows.

When the senior leadership keeps the vision clear and values steadfast, strategies to fulfill the vision will often come from your volunteers.

As senior leaders, continue to teach and model the structure of Exodus 18, 1 Corinthians 12 and Ephesians 4. People will live out a lifestyle asking God what He wants them to do through their passion and talents to bring justice to those who are experiencing injustice.

We use three words at Green Valley to help decide our integrated strategies so they flow out of our clear vision and values:

Dignity: Are there practical, biblical, redemptive ways to offer dignity toward people who are experiencing indignity?

Honor: Are their practical, redemptive ways to bring honor to the people who have been misjudged by the world or the church?

Messy: Are we willing to get messy in areas that the Church has avoided in the past because of the fear of the unknown or the fear of failing?

Dignity
When people's hearts are broken and tender, strategies that flow from the vision usually involve bringing dignity to those labeled "undignified."

Dignity - Noun: The state or quality of being worthy of honor or respect.

What do a widower suffering from Parkinson's, a single woman trying to care for her quadriplegic father and a transition house for girls rescued from sex trafficking have in common?

They were all served by Green Valley Community Church on Saturday mornings by hundreds of volunteers.

Raking, mowing and weeding, painting, roofing, building fences, replacing trim, building and staining of decks, pouring concrete to fit walkers and wheelchairs, cleaning and repairing living rooms and kitchens - This all happened on a Saturday.

Simple, yet profound and life-changing strategies.

What else do these precious people have in common? Most of them have never attended any of our church services. They are the forgotten people our culture so easily throws away.

I am grateful for these Saturdays of service, not just because we get to bless someone who needs help. I am grateful for these days, selfishly, because I think we are the ones most blessed.

When the church offers <u>dignity</u>, it is doing the best it can do!

While these service projects happen all around our community on Saturday mornings, beautiful things happen on our church campus as well.

Around three hundred people eat a warm breakfast, while waiting to pick up a bag of groceries and a bag of vegetables from our church garden to help them get through the week.

Saturday mornings, people receive about 1,500 articles of clothing from our clothing ministry. Items distributed include suits for upcoming job interviews, blankets and shoes for cold winter months and prom dresses for young ladies looking for that special dress to feel dignified at their school dance. The precious people who come on Saturday mornings consist of senior citizens, single parents, families going through difficult financial times and the homeless.

Each Saturday morning, people come through our doors and experience not only physical food but they also experience spiritual, emotional and relational food. They experience words of encouragement and hope and are treated with God's grace.

Simple yet life-changing strategies.
When the church is offering <u>dignity</u>, I think it is at its best!

While this is happening inside our church, every Saturday our garden team shows up to help produce hundreds of pounds of potatoes, squash, tomatoes, carrots, peppers, pumpkins, radishes, cucumbers and much more.

At the same time, other volunteers are cutting and splitting wood so that people will have warm homes during the cold winters. Over the last few years, we have averaged giving away 150 truckloads of wood to the elderly, single moms and to those who cannot afford to heat their homes.

On any given Saturday, hundreds of volunteers make this happen. And, I believe they would tell you it's the best day of their week.

I love my church. We are not perfect, but I see so many volunteers using their time, strengths and resources to bring dignity to those that are overlooked and marginalized.

I see how serving people in tangible, practical ways, in Jesus' name, transforms lives and is changing our community. I see the impact my church has in our community through the selfless acts of offering dignity and I often ask this one question: With around 300,000 churches in the United States, I wonder what our country would look like if every church offered dignity in strategic, simple, humbling, quiet and practical ways?

In the words of Pastor Bill Wilson of Metro Ministries, *"We want God to touch our country, but God is asking us to touch our country."*

Honor

The second word that guides our strategies is the word honor.

Honor - Noun: High respect; esteem. Verb: Regard with deep respect

Are we serving others through our actions in practical, redemptive ways to bring **honor** to the people who have been misjudged by the world or even the church?

Who are the misjudged and how can they find healing?
An abandoned daughter discovers her Heavenly Father.
An angry ex-con encounters authentic friendships.
A controlling mother learns to let go and let God.
A one year clean woman mentors a struggling drug addict.
A relationship destroying alcoholic gains new tools and makes amends.
A recovering sex addict finds new purpose and is set free.
A guilt-ridden religious woman experiences grace.

Who are these people?

These are the people Brennan Manning celebrated when he wrote, *"There is a beautiful transparency to honest disciples who never wear a false face and do not pretend to be anything but who they are."*

These are the people Jesus had in mind when He said, *"I have come to heal the broken-hearted."*

These are the people Jesus said are the greatest because of their humility and commitment to one another.

These are the people the scriptures implore us to honor and respect.

These are the people Jesus would call the Church.

Yet...

These are the people most churches reject, ignore and outsource to other agencies. Most churches marginalize, judge, undervalue and underserve these people. Most churches do not give them honor or respect. These are the people most churches hope go somewhere else.

Yet...

These people bring huge blessings to our church.
These people show us that God is still in the miracle business.
These people show us transparency and bravery.
These people show us that we are all in recovery from something.
These people show us that the ground is level at the foot of the cross.

Why are so many fleeing the church? Because the church has abandoned honor and respect. Because the church has rejected "these people."

These are the very people Jesus said he would judge us by how we treated them. These are the very people Jesus said when we serve and love them, we will be blessed. These are the very people Jesus said when we serve and love them, we serve and love Him.

Too often we want for the world to change when in reality, the Church must change.

Until the Church becomes transparent, inclusive, safe, courageous, messy, grace-filled, humble and willing to sacrifice, we will continue to shrink and lose ground.

Too often we want the world to repent, when it is the Church who must repent. If the Church is not serving and welcoming and honoring and allowing "these people" to lead, then it is really not the Church, but a building. An exclusive club.

At our church, "these people" call themselves "Celebrate Recovery" and they are leading the way toward blessings, miracles, redemption and a rare intimacy with God. I not only honor and respect "these people," I desperately need them because of their inspiration and contagious courage!

Thank you for your example in humility.
Thank you for your leadership in transparency.
Thank you for your commitment to grace.
Thank you for re-introducing us to the presence of God.

When we honor and hold in high "regard with deep respect "these people" we *"will raise up the age-old foundations; you will be called Repairer of Broken Walls, Restorer of Streets with Dwellings."* Isaiah 58:12 (NIV)

May we see a revolution of "these people!"

Messy
The third word that guides our strategies is the word "messy."

Messy - Adjective: The state of disorder, complex, chaotic, unsure.

Are we willing to get **messy** in areas that the church has avoided in the past because of the fear of the unknown or the fear of failure?

Green Valley is a very messy church because God has not asked us to play safe. He has asked us to storm the gates of hell and that can get very chaotic.

Fearless strategies are messy and always need adjustment. You must be willing to learn from failure. In the words of Jim Collins, *"Preserve the core* (vision and values) *while stimulating the progress* (strategies)."

All pastors face the normal everyday pressures of ministry. They face their congregational needs, their community needs and their financial needs.

Who will have the vision and courage and strength to take risks, extending love to a dying world? Who will play it safe, remain comfortable and preserve order?

One of the biggest reasons I see senior leaders, pastors and churches shy away from being trailblazers in their community and world is their fear of messiness. I see individuals and churches doing "fly-by's" past the gates of hell, but not penetrating the gates. Those can be scary, uncertain and messy places and it is easier to play it safe.

One of the most dignifying, honoring, messy ministries we have at Green Valley is our funeral ministry.

I remember meeting with some leaders from a church that wanted to start doing funerals for families in their community. They wanted to see how we were leading this ministry at Green Valley. They seemed very eager to start sharing the love of Jesus during one of the most difficult times for a family.

They were eager to start until we told them we do not charge. And I let them know that when you do funerals for people who do not necessarily know God, it can get a little messy and raw (and entertaining if I might add).

We could see fear spread across their faces. They experienced a complete reversal from "Wouldn't it be nice to do something nice?" to "This looks too scary and messy to even attempt."

You could see them add up the costs, wondering if they could afford it.

You could also see the nervousness of potentially having people stand up during a service and say things that do not quite fit in the category of "church chat."

Then I told them a story that I thought would encourage them but it seemed to create a paralyzing fear in them.

We did a funeral several years ago for a family devastated by the loss of a 43 year old father suddenly killed in an automobile accident. This is a wonderful family—not church goers and a bit rough around the edges. However, for the first time in a long time, they were seeking God during this crisis. Our funeral team loved them and didn't judge their language as they grieved honestly. The service went well. Open mic time had some interesting language but no damage done. During the reception, while around 100 people were eating and crying and talking and laughing and remembering stories about this father, the family asked us if we could put in a DVD of some pictures and video that they didn't play during the service. We said "of course" (it seemed like a pretty benign request). The DVD started with pictures of birthday parties, fishing trips, camping and vacations, when suddenly a stripper at a bachelor party appeared on screen and we froze. By the way, we have a new policy: Do not show a DVD without looking at it first! Before we could do anything about it, the picture changed and it went back to pictures of birthday parties, family gatherings and hunting trips - but it certainly surprised us all. One of the best lines of all time came from one of our funeral ministry volunteer leaders who is in her seventies. When she saw the picture, she said, "Well, this is why we do what we do." I love her! She gets it.

My point is, storming the gates of hell is messy and we can't let fear stop us from doing the right thing.

Fear of lack of resources can be messy to our **comfort** but God asks us to trust the One who owns cattle on a thousand hills. Fear of what people will think can be messy to our **status**, but God asks us to live only to please Him.

Fear of being around people that are different than us can be messy to our **prejudices**, but God reminds us that they are all precious and redeemable in His sight.

Fear of failure can be messy to our **ego**, but God reminds us that a righteous man falls down seven times but gets back up again.

Fear of danger can be messy to our **sterilized, safe lifestyles**, but God reminds us that even though we walk through the valley of the shadow of death, he will be with us. Many churches in California stopped going down to Mexico to help orphaned children because they feared drug shootings along the border.

Fear of messiness stops us from doing great things.
Fear of messiness stops us from seeing miracles.

I am so glad Jesus didn't let fear of the messiness of the crucifixion stop him from going to the cross.

Orphans, widows, the hungry, the abused and those that don't know about the love of God are hoping churches won't be paralyzed by the fear of messiness.

When Jesus said we should die so we could live, sometimes that means literally. We like metaphors, but not literal translations when it comes to giving our lives up as a fragrant offering for the work of God.

What challenges, visions and dreams are you facing that God wants you to do? Is the messiness allowing fear to control you?

You can't remove all the risks out of society. Ministry and life are messy because people are messy but we need to love them anyway.

Dignity

Honor

Messy

When your vision and values are clear and you are resolved to storm the gates of hell, these words will identify and define your strategies.

A LEADER'S LAMENT

Sometimes I care too much, my ego trumps reason
Sometimes I don't care enough, it depends on the season
I beat the drum often, not wanting others to forget
Not sharing in my passion, they insincerely acquiesce

Only a few things matter, yet my brain is scattered
One word of criticism, and my worth is shattered
When it comes to living, when it comes to teamwork
Everyone talks the talk, but the walk is misgiving

"We" are stronger than "I", as long as "I" gets the credit
My humility most impressive, I'll tell you all about it
I want the truth, desperately seeking transparency
Yet words are guarded, dishonesty flowered deceptively

I'm here for you, I've got your back
I believe in you, there's nothing I lack
Unless someone disagrees, unless someone moans
Then I need to step away, I need courage on loan

A fish out of water, is a fish out of air
I have something in common, it's something I share
Take care of my cause, take care of my needs
Then I'll let people know, you are a wise man who leads

But leading isn't popularity, it isn't first to please
It isn't taking polls, it's not putting people at ease
It means having deep convictions, having secure beliefs
It means staying true to course, not taking relief

The hill I climb is lonely, often feeling stranded
The hill I climb is barren, often taken for granted
The hill I climb is noble, the hill I climb is inspiring
As long as it does not get in the way of your living

Females raped and murdered, where is the rage?
It seems important, but message gets back page
The Church is the answer, the message of justice we bring
But the words get muted, arguing over the songs we sing

Children die before 5, $20 is the solution
My debit card is low, comfort my main concern
I have the money, but I'm keeping up with the Jones'
Car, House, Boat, busy paying off the loans'

The world needs billions, seems overwhelming
Billions would not compare, if Christians were tithing
I can't do it all, but I can open the door
If I learn to say "No", I can do so much more

Boys without role models, absent of fathers
They are not on my block, so why even bother
But the needs are great, the opportunities do not lack
I am the change I pray for, but my schedule is packed

Options are good, until there are too many
Poverty cries out, "I don't have any"
America the beautiful, everyone given equal chance
Unless born in the hood, equality becomes a fat chance

More concerned about position, more about my security
My dreams are much more daring, as I live in my safety
Been told to be quiet, told "balance" is for the wise
There's no more heroes, "well rounded" is our demise

I check my heart, I check by pride
I check my will, putting desires aside
I live in abundance, my challenges are few
When I say I have problems, I ask, "Compared to who?"

People want the world to be like them
I say, they should want the world to be like Him
As soon as I say my theology is a lock
I have just put God right in a box

My faith is bigger than Republican or Democrat
My faith is stronger than where the world is at
Jesus created this world, then gave his life
He asks me to love this world, then give up my life

Sometimes I care too much, my ego trumps reason
Sometimes I don't care enough, it depends on the season
But one thing I know, one thing I am sure
That loving orphans and widows is a religion that's pure!

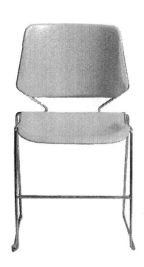

MANDATE 5

Clear Evidence of Authentic
Transformation of Volunteers

Mandate 5
Clear Evidence of Authentic Transformation of Volunteers

"I alone cannot change in the world, but I can cast a stone across the waters to create many ripples."
Mother Theresa

"Then he said to his disciples, The harvest is plentiful but the workers are few."
Matthew 9:35-37 (NIV)

You have to go out, but you don't have to come back.

On Nantucket Island, there is a little museum devoted to a volunteer organization formed centuries ago. In those days, travel by sea posed extreme danger. Because of storms in the Atlantic along the rocky coast of Massachusetts, many crews and passengers drowned within a mile or so of land.

So a group of volunteers went into the life-saving business. They banded together to form what they named "the Humane Society."

These people built little huts along the shore. They had people watching the sea constantly. Whenever a ship went down, they sounded the alarm, and the Humane Society would devote their full attention to save every life they could.

They put themselves at risk because they prized human life—no money or fame involved. In fact they adopted the motto, "You have to go out, but you don't have to come back." Not a great recruiting slogan, is it? These brave people risked everything—even their lives—to save people they never met.

But over time, things changed.

After a while, the U.S. Coast Guard took over the task of rescue. Eventually, they lived by the idea, "Let the professionals do it. They're better trained. They get paid for it."

Volunteers stopped searching the coastlines for ships in danger. They stopped sending teams out to rescue drowning people.

Yet, a strange thing happened. They couldn't bring themselves to disband. The life-saving society still exists. The members meet every once in awhile to have dinners. They are just not in the life-saving business anymore.

Two thousand years ago, a band of rag-tag followers of Jesus began to meet regularly to pray and strategize how they could rescue a shipwrecked world.

It was a calling they took seriously.

Their motto was, "You have to go out, but you don't have to come back."

They embraced this slogan as you see by the writing in Acts, "...the Lord added to the church daily those who were being saved." (NKJV)

Followers of Jesus had reputations for adopting abandoned children, serving the poor, fighting and dying for justice, and staying in plague-filled cities to care for the sick. Others fled to safe places. Rulers and governments found themselves intrigued, confused and threatened by the Christians' willingness to give their life for others.

The early Church left a permanent mark in the secular history books of the day. What will history write about today's Church? Was it willing to go out, with little concern for coming back? Or was it judgmental, exclusive, irrelevant, fearful, professionalized? After getting out of the life-saving arena, did the Church just continue to have meetings not worth mentioning in history books?

Management consultant and author Peter Drucker says, "It's the human propensity to start with a clear vision and to get it muddied up along the way. It's just kind of what happens to human beings in organizations."

How badly the Church is missed in our culture. Yet there seems to be a church on every corner. How can the Church be missed when it is all around us?

The prophet Isaiah said that when the Church is busy with meetings it becomes powerless.

The power of the Church comes from caring for the poor, feeding the hungry, fighting injustice, and protecting widows and orphans. The impact of the church is not predicated on frequency of meetings and the eloquent nature of its rhetoric. Its impact is not determined by a nice, accessible location. The impact of the church has to do with its willingness to lay its life down for a ship-wrecked world.

When the church begins to re-live the motto, "You have to go out, but you don't have to come back", it will become relevant once again.

There are many ways to evaluate whether volunteers in our church are growing, but these three obvious points come to mind:

Fear is replaced by contagious courage.
Prayer transitions from mere words to heroic action.
God's Kingdom replaces our temporary kingdoms.

Fear

One of the biggest evidences of a transformed pastor and congregation is that power, love and a sound mind replace fear.

My son went to college in Southern California and worked for a grocery store chain. Late one night, a man came running into the store past my son. He turned around to face my son, about twenty feet away, and started shooting at him. The man was actually shooting at a policeman who had run into the store, but the policeman was right behind my son. My son was in the line of fire.

He dove to the left to avoid the bullets, but the policeman dove to the left also. A Doritos display stood between the shooter and my son so shards of nacho cheese Doritos flew everywhere. The sliding glass doors at the front of the store shattered from the bullets.

My son said everything moved in slow motion and the noise was deafening. Long story short, my son (who we now call Superman) moved faster than the speeding bullets. He avoided the bullets, while the policeman began to shoot back and eventually shot the man. My son was fine, but he had to sit in the police station all night giving reports about what he saw. I tell you this story because that night my son met a couple in the police station that he will never forget.

This couple was from the state of Washington and the husband taught accounting at Washington State. They were Christ followers. The Christian university in southern California where my son attends school wanted to hire him. The man wanted to take the job, but his wife was nervous about moving to California because it seemed like a dangerous, wild kind of place.

The University said, "Why don't you come down and just check out the place." They did. They landed at the airport and drove to check into their hotel. On the way they decided to stop by a local grocery store to pick up some snacks.

When they drove in front of the store, bullets started hitting the side of their rental car. Yes, the same bullets my son was avoiding inside. This couple had been in California for 2 hours and their worst fears were coming true.They had become a part of a Hollywood movie.

The couple came out unharmed, but they were required to go to the police station to tell their story and this is when their paths crossed with my son. After they told him the story, my son thought, "Well, this is the last time they will ever come to California." After giving reports on what they saw, everyone went their separate ways. About three months later, my son was working one late night at the grocery store and he turned around and saw this woman from Washington. Bonded by flying bullets, my son gave her a big hug and asked her what she was doing there and she said that they decided to take the job and move to California.

She told my son, "We are not going to let some random act of violence keep us from doing what God wants us to do. We are not going to let fear have the last word!" I love that couple!

How can we start a new revolution of courage? How can churches turn from playing it safe to "storming the gates"? The answer is simple. Psalm 56:3 says, *"When I am afraid, I will put my confidence in God. Yes, I will trust the promises of God."*

"I put my confidence in God." He does not say, "I'm not afraid." He is afraid. Courage is moving ahead in spite of your fear. The courageous person is scared to death and does it anyway. Paul wrote *"I have the strength to face*

all conditions by the power that Christ gives me." That's what it means to live by faith. You feel the fear and you do it anyway. The Israelites stood at the Red Sea; God did not take them around the Red Sea. He didn't build a bridge over the Red Sea. He took them through the Red Sea.

They could have stood on the sidelines for the rest of their lives, saying, "We believe God is going to save us." But it wasn't until they stepped into the water that it started happening. Moses held up his staff and said, "Move in. Get going." You move against your fear. You do the thing you fear the most. That's courage.

As my good friend Bonnie Belzer says, *"If you aren't living life on the edge, you are taking up too much space."*

When volunteers become ministers of grace, resulting in a deep, personal ownership of their faith, fearless generosity, humility to work as a team and a transparent soul, they become free to live the life God has called them towards.

The apostle Paul wrote, *"Perfect love casts out fear."* (NKJV)

The closer we get to that perfect love and His heart and mission (Isaiah 58, Proverbs 31:8-9, Luke 4:18-19, Matthew 25, James 1:27) the less we will allow fear to stop us from storming the gates of hell.

There is a lot of "storming" at Green Valley these days. I love the fearlessness of Green Valley volunteers. You know that your volunteers are transforming when faith and courage replace debilitating fear.

Prayer

A second evidence of transformation is the concrete connection between deep prayer and courageous action. Prayer becomes the power to faithful, practical service and mind-boggling miracles.

Prayer is not the end but the beginning of great things.

One of the most counter-intuitive moments in scripture comes when the children of Israel are trapped between Pharaoh's army and the Red Sea. The people panicked. They took out their anger on Moses, asked why he had them escape just to die and told him they would rather be slaves in Egypt than slaughtered in the desert!

It wasn't a great "leadership moment" for Moses.

On top of their anger, Moses gives some advice and guidance that seems right initially, but he gets it totally wrong. He tells them, *"Don't be afraid. Just stand still and watch the LORD rescue you today."* Exodus 14:13 (NLT)

Sounds like good advice and great faith, doesn't it?
We hear this advice all the time:

"Don't be afraid. Stand still and the Lord will rescue us from this sad world."
"Don't be afraid. Stand still and the Lord will take care of the poor."
"Don't be afraid. Stand still and the Lord will bless us and give us the desires of our heart."
"Don't be afraid. Stand still and the Lord will take care of our needs."

This was God's response to Moses' bad advice. He said, *"Quit praying and get the people moving! Forward, march!"* Exodus 14:15 (TLB)

Now, I grew up in church and I never heard one sermon where the pastor told us to quit praying. In fact it seemed like all we did was pray.

We prayed for Jesus to come back.
We prayed that evil people would get their due.
We prayed that we would not get stained by an immoral world.
We prayed for who would become president.
We prayed that God would bless us financially.
We prayed that other denominations would become holy like us.
We even prayed for people less fortunate than us.

We prayed, went home for a week, and then came back and prayed again.

We prayed often, eloquently.

Our church could win a prayer contest. We even had a chapel called the "House of Prayer."

Now don't get me wrong, I am all for prayer.
Prayer is where I gain my intimacy with God.
Prayer is where I get the power to live.
Prayer is where I gain wisdom.

Prayer is where I find peace.
Prayer is where I experience rest.
Prayer is the foundation to my life in faith.

So why did God tell Moses to quit praying and get moving?

Here is my theory. Many times prayer is an excuse to not do something that we already know God wants us to do.

There are many things we don't have to pray about.
Serving the poor.
Caring for orphans.
Taking care of widows.
Being a father to the fatherless.
Feeding the hungry.
Sheltering the homeless.
Clothing the naked.
Forgiving our enemy.
Rescuing young women and children who are sex trafficked.
Fighting injustice.

We don't have to pray and ask whether or not God wills these things. In fact, it is possible to actually pray more while moving away from God.

God spoke through the prophet Isaiah and said, *"When you lift up your hands in prayer, I will not look. Though you offer many prayers, I will not listen...Learn to do good. Seek justice. Helped the oppressed. Defend the cause of orphans. Fight for the rights of widows."* Isaiah 1:15,17 (NLT)

Don't get me wrong. I believe deeply in prayer!

But don't let prayer become an excuse to not do what God is asking you to do. Prayer is not the end, but the beginning to an action of love and justice.

I would like to challenge the American Church to pray less and do more. Let me explain - pray through all things but don't let prayer stop you from the actions God is telling you to take. Don't let prayer be an excuse for inactivity or causing you to wait to help someone who you know needs your assistance. "Let me pray about that" is a common phrase used to stall in response to a need because of fear.

I believe God is challenging the church today to:
Get out of our prayer meetings and go help someone. Leave our worship services and feed someone. Stop talking about the poor and invite the homeless into our services. Stop building bigger buildings and spend more money on local and global missions. Stop looking the other way and sponsor children in poverty stricken countries. Cancel your women's teas and your men's breakfasts and rebuild a widow's home or mentor a child who has no father.

Stop praying for blessings and help those who God has asked us very clearly to help, because that is where the blessings are!

God has made it very plain what he expects us to do.

"He has shown you, O man, what is good;
And what does the Lord require of you But to do justly,
To love mercy, And to walk humbly with your God?"
Micah 6:8 (NKJV)

I think He would go on to say, "And while you are doing those things, pray! Pray hard, pray often. I will give you the strength and the wisdom and courage to shine your light and "storm the gates" of poverty, hopelessness and loneliness. The world will be drawn to Me through your actions and the world will know that I am love."

What happened when God told Moses to quit praying and get moving?
They experienced a miracle.
May the Church do the same!

"Witness the fact that in the Lord's Prayer, the first
petition is for daily bread. No one can worship God or
love his neighbor on an empty stomach."
Woodrow Wilson

"I prayed for twenty years but received no answer
until I prayed with my legs."
Frederick Douglass

"Before we can pray, "Lord, Thy Kingdom come,"
we must be willing to pray, "My Kingdom go."
Alan Redpath — British Evangelist and Author

"Prayer begets faith, faith begets love,
and love begets service on behalf of the poor."
Mother Teresa

These days at Green Valley, we focus on prayers that lead to a deeper faith. This leads to a deeper love for God, which has led to a deeper love and a high commitment to serve the poor.

God's Kingdom
Clear evidence of authentic transformation comes when courage replaces fear; prayer begets action towards the poor and finally when people begin to replace their small kingdom mindset with God's Kingdom mindset.

Another way to say it is: there is a continual shifting from a cultural, political, divided, exclusive, nationalistic, small kingdom kind of faith toward a global, inclusive, expansive, compassionate, awe-inspiring, God-kingdom kind of faith.

God in a Box
Henri Nouwen, author of The Wounded Healer, said, *"We cannot expect God to speak to us in our narrow corridor of thinking. As scripture shows us, He may speak to us through a saint or a sinner. Through a conservative or a liberal. Through a man or a woman – or a young child. Through an old person or a young person. Through an educated or an illiterate person... Through a local person or a foreigner. We have at all times to be ready to listen with an unprejudiced mind and heart."*

I was thinking about my life and how God speaks to me through so many diverse voices, with differing opinions and backgrounds. Each one compels me closer to the heart of Jesus.

With help from a liberal sociologist named Tony Campolo, along with a conservative preacher named Franklin Graham, my heart breaks for the poor.

From an Irish rock star named Bono to an agnostic brilliant business man named Bill Gates, my urgency to end extreme poverty has increased.

Through messages from an alcoholic priest named Brennan Manning and a 90-year-old saint named Mother Rose, I am overwhelmed by the gift of Grace.

From an African American, born in the ghetto, named Ricky Bolden, to a 75 year old, rich white man named Doug Coe, I will forever be burdened and invested in the inner city.

From a conservative business man named Jim Copeland to a more liberal mother committed to public health around the world, named Kim Dickson, my life has refocused on the rights of children and women around the world.

From an Albanian Roman Catholic nun named Mother Teresa to a cancer research doctor named Scott Todd, I am compelled to look extreme poverty in the face and defeat it.

I have a very close friend who is gay and whenever I am with him, I leave having a deeper passion to follow Jesus. I find my heart more convicted to serve the marginalized and forgotten in my community.

The important question for people of faith today is: Can we see past the surface, the titles, the labels and see the wisdom underneath?

When John the Baptist came to proclaim the coming of the Messiah, he was described as a locust-eating, leather- wearing, adultery-condemning prophet.

When Jesus walked this earth, he was described as a party-going, wine-making, heart-healing, sin-forgiving Savior.

John would have been labeled a conservative and Jesus would have been labeled a liberal.

Jesus told the Pharisees, *"'We played the flute for you, And you did not dance; We mourned to you, And you did not weep.' For John the Baptist came neither eating bread nor drinking wine, and you say, 'He has a demon.' The Son of Man has come eating and drinking, and you say, 'Look, a glutton and a winebibber, a friend of tax collectors and sinners!'"* Luke 7:32-34 (NKJV)

The gospel came looking two different ways, but they could not see it. Why? Because the Pharisees had put God in a box.

The strength of faith is the diversity of God's wisdom. That is why people should travel, to see the image and creativity and vastness of God.

The Pharisees are not the only ones who have put God in a box. In America, we are in that danger today.

In order for our faith to be rich and our hearts to remain soft and pliable, we must continue to be overwhelmed by the vastness of God.

Jesus was not an American. He was not a Californian. He was not a Republican or a Democrat. He was not a Presbyterian, Methodist, Pentecostal or Baptist. He was not a member of the NRA, Greenpeace or the local Moose lodge. He did not have a preference of musical worship style, because his worship had to do with spirit and truth. He was anti-revenge and anti-hate.

He said, *"Give to Caesar what is Caesar's, and give to God what is God's!"*

He was the creator of the universe and it was his idea to make the stars and the moon and the seas and the mountains. Red, brown, yellow, black and white, they are all equally precious in his sight. Every color, creed and culture has part of his image.

He loves our enemies and he prays that the terrorist will find salvation like the terrorist Saul who became a champion of grace. He loves you even when you walk away. He loves me even when I choose my own way.

Jesus' Kingdom is bigger than any of our big ideas and heaven will be a much different place than our middle class, American ideas.

When Peter quotes the Prophet Joel in Acts 2 and says, *"All who call on the name of the Lord will be saved."* He meant ALL!

It is Jesus + nothing!
Not Jesus + politics.
Not Jesus + denomination.
Not Jesus + lifestyle.
Not Jesus + American.

Let us allow Jesus to be bigger than any of our big ideas and run towards his radical, counter-intuitive, compassionate Grace.

AUTHENTIC TRANSFORMATION:
Fear moving toward courage.
Prayer moving toward action.
Small kingdom moving toward God's Kingdom.

MANDATE 6

Measurable, Effective "Isaiah 58" Success
in the Church and Community

Mandate 6
Measurable, Effective "Isaiah 58" Success
in the Church and Community

> "Try not to become a man of success.
> Rather become a man of value."
> **Albert Einstein**

> "Our greatest fear should not be of failure but of
> succeeding at things in life that don't really matter."
> **Francis Chan - Author of Crazy Love**

The Definition of Success
God's definition of success is different than mine.

Those of us who call ourselves believers are still trying to live out the world's definition of success most of the time. We expect that giving our lives to God will save our souls, while our American dream will be enhanced because God is on our side.

Churches proclaim the words of Jesus, "You have to lose your life to gain it," but they still define success as corporations define success.

How many people attend?
How much money comes in?
How large is the building?
How do we compare to other churches?

The apostle Paul reminds us that Jesus showed us what the true definition of success is. "*Who, being in very nature God, did not consider equality with God something to be used to his own advantage; rather, he made himself nothing by taking the very nature of a servant, being made in human likeness. And being found in appearance as a man, he humbled himself by becoming obedient to death—even death on a cross!*" Philippians 2:6-8 (NIV)

The older I get, the more I realize that the truly successful people in this world will never be recognized this side of Heaven.

I think of a man I know, an 85 year old widower who lost the love of his life years ago. He quietly serves the poor in his local town, by serving meals to the hungry, delivering groceries to the elderly and financially sponsoring 22 Compassion International children from all over the world. He will never get on CNN, yet he is one of the most successful people I have ever known.

I think of a woman I know, who has suffered much tragedy in her life, her only son murdered. She is helping people who are experiencing severe loss, helping them heal and find hope. She will not become rich by doing this, though there is a richness she is experiencing that cannot be explained. She is one of the most successful people I have ever known.

I think of a couple who lost their son to drugs. As they are raising their beautiful granddaughter, they are helping broken young people move away from the destruction of drugs and toward hope and God's grace. They will not get their son back this side of Heaven, but his legacy will now be about the saving of hundreds of lives from the destruction of addiction. They are two of the most successful people I have ever known.

Life brings pain.

God takes ashes and makes them beautiful. God takes darkness and tells us to hang on because the morning promises joy. God says in this life there will be tears, sorrow and loss but one day that will cease.

God redefines success.

"We fail to see the place of suffering in the broader scheme of things. We fail to see that suffering is an inevitable dimension of life. Because we have lost perspective, we fail to see that unless one is willing to accept suffering properly, he or she is really refusing to continue in the quest for maturity. To refuse suffering is to refuse personal growth."
Henri J.M. Nouwen

Refusing personal growth keeps us from true success.

One thing concerning me about the American Church is that it is possible to be "popular" without being "relevant". God's definition of success states that however unpopular and uncomfortable the cross is, it is the most relevant gift the universe has ever received.

What is truly relevant? Risking our lives feeding empty bellies; rescuing children out of the dungeons of trafficking; inviting people to the Kingdom party who believe they have nothing to offer, because everyone has something to offer; praying for, forgiving and loving our enemies; giving God our first 10%, putting others before us, investing in the next generation where it is hard to see instant results.

The true definition of success is far more about relevancy than popularity. As a pastor or senior leader of your church or organization, you must determine what a "win" is in your ministry and then find practical, consistent ways to measure it. Below are seven ways Green Valley measures effective "Isaiah 58" outcomes and success:

1. People who were broken and have found healing are now helping others.

2. People's hearts are growing in generosity.

3. People are developing gratitude and their lifestyles are moving towards focused simplicity.

4. Our non-churched community trusts us to help them during difficult times in their lives.

5. People build relationships with the hungry, the homeless and the marginalized.

6. We have a growing sense of adventure, where people allow themselves to live on the edge of faith.

7. We have a reputation for accepting rather than judging.

Let's look at each one in detail.

Measure of Effectiveness
#1: People who were broken have found healing are now helping others.

*"He comforts us in all our troubles so that we can comfort others.
When they are troubled, we will be able to give them
the same comfort God has given us."*
2 Corinthians 1:4 (NLT)

Vanessa's Story:

Vanessa was born into a broken world on Nov. 3, 1989. She was loved, but she didn't love herself. When she was two, her father died in a motorcycle accident in Southern California. Her mother was 21 years old with two small children, no job, no education. Life became chaotic for this young mom. Sadness, anger and regret filled their lives, though no one ever talked about it.

Vanessa learned at a very early age to stuff deep hurts and play the part of a happy kid. She played a lot of make believe, numbing herself to the reality of sadness, loneliness, pain and guilt. She also coped by binge-eating and hurting herself.

Vanessa and her family went to church occasionally but her perception of God was that He had a lot of rules that would send her straight to hell... The whole church thing just wasn't appealing," she told me. Her mother met a man and the family moved to Colorado. Vanessa felt like she was starting a new life with a new dad.

Everything seemed perfect until at age 10, when she was molested by a neighbor. She never told anyone about it, not realizing that anything out of the ordinary happened. Her mom got engaged, but then was diagnosed with cancer. Vanessa's mom's new fiancé could not face this storm so he left. Once again, Vanessa faced abandonment.

While her mom was getting medical treatment, Vanessa and her sister would stay up all night to drink alcohol and smoke marijuana. They moved back to California and their partying intensified. Her life was spinning out of control when she entered high school, although on the surface you would not know.

She took honors classes receiving high grades. She played water polo and was on the swim team. She, starred in school plays, took dance class, was involved in journalism, worked as statistician for the wrestling team and assisted with school rallies. She was a highly successful — or so it appeared.

But excessive drinking, smoking weed and stealing prescription drugs happened every day. Vanessa began to sell marijuana which led to her arrest and doing community service.

Her sophomore year she had a miscarriage. Then things got worse. She discovered the drug of her choice. Methamphetamine.

While still putting on a good show on the outside, her mom caught her doing meth. This is when her mom finally told Vanessa about the night her father died. She had caught him smoking meth and kicked her dad out of the house. He crashed his motorcycle that night. Feeling deceived, Vanessa ran away and did not finish the last 2 months of school.

Her mother reported her missing (thus violating her probation) and she was arrested and spent 2 1/2 months in jail—sober. When she got out, she started college with great intentions but quickly re-started the cycle of drinking and drugs.

"My disease was much stronger than my ambition."

Vanessa jumped around from one high to another and ended up in Las Vegas where her dad's friend lived. She moved in with this older man and, she said *"I found my usual low-life crowd and began selling weed, coke and Ecstasy. I was then introduced to the pimp and prostitution game. They appeared to have it all. Little did I know they were just great actresses. I got myself a pimp who was also a drug dealer."*

"That day, I sold my soul."

Things went from bad to violent to worse and Vanessa eventually left her pimp but she kept selling drugs and was re-introduced to meth. 6 months later - smoking meth daily - she lost everything. She cut off her long, beautiful hair and went into seclusion. Her mom called the morgue often to find out if she was alive.

"The toxins of the drugs were seeping out of my pores. I would pick at my skin all over my body. My once flawless complexion was constantly covered in sores. I spent my 21st birthday getting high in a closet."

On the night of November 17, 2010, someone turned Vanessa in on a $10,000 bounty. It saved her life.

She got lost in the system, which was a blessing in disguise. For 21 days she reflected on her life and her choices. *"I looked into the foggy jail mirror and saw a grimy creature I didn't recognize. God told me in a gentle whisper, 'This is not what I want for you. This is not who you are.'"*

Under house arrest, she immersed herself into recovery and followed the rules like her life depended on it. And it did.

"One day, as I was contemplating what the God of my understanding was to me, Jesus appeared. I have always been a cloud watcher. There He was wearing the crown of thorns, like an image I'd had on a postcard as a child. He was smiling at me and I could see that He was so proud. I had more hope that evening than any other moment of my entire life!"

Vanessa learned that the root of her disease lies in obsession, compulsion, self-centeredness and lack of faith. She moved to California and arrived in Placerville with a new ankle monitor.

Her mom mentioned that her church, Green Valley, offered several recovery groups. Vanessa thought, *"Oh great! They are going to shove religion down my throat."*

At a Celebrate Recovery meeting that evening, Vanessa experienced something she had not experienced before.

"That first night at Celebrate Recovery, I felt warmth and a hope I didn't recognize. Everyone was so welcoming and loving.I began to attend church services and I eventually started volunteering. I soon realized that Green Valley Community Church was not a religious church about judgment or being better than others, but it was a Jesus church about relationships and acceptance. I had finally found home. I learned that God is a father to the fatherless. He offers grace and forgiveness and peace. I began to like myself. I got off house arrest. I got to flip a sign at Easter reading 'Road to Hell' as my old life and 'Road to Recovery' as my new life."

Vanessa is an inspiration and a miracle and now helps young people recover from their hurts and bad habits. Celebrate Recovery and the church's commitment to help those dealing with hurts, hang-ups and habits has once again drawn us very close to the heart of God.

Jesus stated that he clearly came to *"Heal the brokenhearted and proclaim liberty to the captives."* Luke 4:18 (NKJV)

When people say that God doesn't do miracles anymore, you can bet that they have never participated in Celebrate Recovery. Our Celebrate Recovery program started with a couple who was rejected by another church when they wanted to start the program. The church told them that they weren't sure they wanted people with serious issues and addictions coming into their church. Their sad loss was our gain.

Celebrate Recovery started small and as the leadership grew, so did the program. Eight years later, hundreds have overcome addictions, found healing and God which led to choosing to be baptized. When you go to a Celebrate Recovery service, you experience real church. Each service includes celebration, safe relationships, honest assessment, humbling confession, complete transparency and a contagious feeling of freedom and purpose.

We also host "The Landing" which is Celebrate Recovery for teenage and college students. It is a safe landing place for students to come and heal, build healthy relationships and start good habits.

Every church should help people overcome.

Vanessa's life scripture is from the book of Lamentations where the prophet Jeremiah says, *"I'll never forget the trouble, the utter lostness, the taste of ashes, the poison I've swallowed. I remember it all—oh, how well I remember—the feeling of hitting the bottom. But there's one other thing I remember, and remembering, I keep a grip on hope: God's loyal love couldn't have run out, his merciful love couldn't have dried up. They're created new every morning. How great Your faithfulness! I'm sticking with God (I say it over and over). He's all I've got left."* Lamentations 3:20-24 (MSG)

A clear way to measure whether your church is living out the true Isaiah 58 fast is when people who have experienced healing through difficulties are now deeply committed to helping others.

It's people like:

Barbara Tankersley, whose son was murdered in a random drive-by shooting, leads our Grief Share program.

Mike and Mavis Manthe, whose son became a cocaine addict, walked alongside him through recovery and now lead Celebrate Recovery.

Amelia Cogburn, who as a young mom, experienced personal addictions and living with an abusive husband, is living out her sobriety while leading a single moms' support group.

"If you're in the luckiest 1% of humanity, you owe it to the rest of humanity to think about the other 99%."
Warren Buffett

I know some pastors and leaders are afraid to dedicate a large amount of their focus and energies towards the poor. The poor cannot give back, so it is easy to focus on and cater to those with resources because they help pay the bills. I know that may sound cynical, but it is more truthful than cynical.

If we serve, invite, welcome, honor and bring dignity to the poor, and they start coming to our services, will it scare away the middle class or the wealthy? Yes, it will. But those you lose are not part of the vision. Those who stay will meet Jesus in disguise and grow more generous hearts.

When new people come who have given up on the church and see your focus on serving the poor, they will give, not out of obligation but out of an opportunity to be a part of something great.

Green Valley is not a rich church. Green Valley is a generous church and generosity begets generosity. The generosity and giving at Green Valley has increased in proportion to the amount of focus and resources we positioned to serve and love the poor.

One of the fruits of God breaking our hearts for the poor is a more generous, sacrificial heart.

An example of this at Green Valley occurred on a weekend in the middle of August 2013. In the heat of the summer, we dedicated an entire weekend to learning about the need for safe water in developing countries. The number one reason children die in developing countries is the lack of safe, clean water.

Compassion International has a filter available for purchase that provides a family, safe, clean water for a lifetime. The local Compassion churches distribute them to families who need it the most. They say when you buy a filter, you provide safe water for at least 10 people because of the sharing that occurs within the villages.

I went to my Board of Directors and asked them if we could spend an entire weekend talking about safe water and the opportunities to save lives. I proposed to ask if each family would buy one water filter. I admitted that this might decrease our normal offerings and August might turn into a tough financial month for our church. However, it seemed like it was something we needed to do to trust and honor God. Without hesitation, my Board looked at me and agreed, "Of Course, we have to do it!"

That weekend, Green Valley families bought over 900 water filters. 900 filters at $55 each. You do the math. Amazingly, our normal offerings were larger than normal also! This remains one of my favorite weekends ever at Green Valley.

Generosity begets generosity.

Measure of Effectiveness
#3: People are developing gratitude and their lifestyles are moving towards focused simplicity.

Eldon Bough was born on February 21, 1927 and he enjoyed a wonderful marriage with Betty, his beautiful bride, for 56 years, 3 months and 1 day. Eldon grew up in a twisted, religious, controlling, abusive family and only knew the God of anger, fear and retribution. As he grew into adulthood, bitterness, anger and a separation from God marked his life. In his 40's, he discovered the God of grace and everything changed. Gratitude and generosity replaced the anger and bitterness. Overwhelmed by this forgiveness and newfound love from God, Eldon's life shows what Jesus meant when he said, *"If you want to gain your life you must lost it,"* and *"You are more blessed when you are giving rather than receiving."*

Eldon serves as a volunteer with Meals on Wheels, delivering over 100,000 meals, often to seniors younger than he is. Eldon serves every Saturday morning at our Common Ground food and clothing giveaway where he pushes shopping carts full of groceries to cars for our guests. In his late 80's, he pushes full carts for 2-3 hours every Saturday in all kinds of weather. Eldon sponsors 22 children through Compassion International and writes to each one every month.

Eldon believes deeply in tithing and supporting his local church. Eldon gives out of gratitude and would tell you he is not in debt because of biblical financial principles. With all the children he sponsors and the generosity of his giving beyond the 10% tithe, he tells me he has plenty of money at the end of the month and is constantly looking at new opportunities to give. Eldon was an elementary school teacher and lives on a retired teacher's pension.

"If you help the poor, you are lending to the LORD
- and he will repay you!"
Proverbs 19:17 (NLT)

Measure of Effectiveness
#4: Our non-churched community trusts us to
help them during difficult times in their lives.

Paul's instruction to "...mourn with those who mourn," did not have a caveat to only mourn with those who believe the same way you do or behave the same way you do.

When Jesus came to heal the broken-hearted, most of those broken-hearted did not know who he was. As the church, we are to help heal a hurting world that does not know the hope of grace or the good news of Jesus.

We average over 50 funerals a year at Green Valley Community Church. 90% of them are for people who do not belong to a church and are either unsure of or far from faith.

This is what Green Valley's funeral and grieving ministries look like:

The family and friends who have experienced loss sit with staff and volunteers to plan the service. The church offers everything they need: live music, pictures, DVD production, food planning and Grief Share options.

When the service happens, all the family has to do is celebrate a life and grieve a loss. They do not have to worry about any of the details, so they can be there in the moment with the freedom to mourn. After the service, the family and friends move to our café for a meal and time to share stories. The healing of sad hearts begins.

We have seen miracles happen in that café. Family members who have not spoken in years reconnect and are reconciled. After the service, we offer a weekly Grief Share class, to teach healthy grieving and provide new friendships. Again 90% of our funerals are for people not connected to a church.

And we charge nothing. Every church should do this!

It is one of the most difficult and blessed things we do. But let me warn you, as I shared before, grace is messy! And let me warn you, when a church begins to do this, it will never be the same. You will never want to go back! Every funeral brings heartbreak and healing. Hurt and hope. Loss and redemption. This is a ministry very close to the heart of God.

If you want to reach out to your community then lovingly and patiently mourn with those who grieve, especially those who are far from God. This act of compassion will change them, change you and it will change your church.

Measure of Effectiveness
#5: People build relationships with the hungry, the homeless and the marginalized.

"Is it not to share your bread with the hungry and bring the homeless poor into your house; when you see the naked, to cover him, and not to hide yourself from your own flesh?"
Isaiah 58:7 (ESV)

Becky's Story:
"I thought Heaven was a home, family and a white picket fence. I didn't know what "steadfast" and "true" meant.

Like so many others, I was abused both physically and sexually as a child. At 17, I became pregnant with my first child. I was able to dodge the bullet of alcohol and substance abuse, at least for a time. I married and tried my best to embrace the Christian lifestyle. Still broken inside, I managed to fake it for eight years but like all illusions, my image gradually started to dissolve and fail. Without any real relationship with Jesus, my marriage fell apart and my life spiraled out of control.

At 28, I became a drug addict to numb my pain. I was so lost. My life continued to ebb and flow. I tried to survive on self-will, never quite understanding what a real relationship with Jesus looked like. I went to churches and talked to many Christians, always listening and waiting for someone to let loose with the big secret. I was always wondering, "How do I make God love me?"

My mother fell ill and I ended up caring for her for 6 years, trying to will her to stay alive.

I ended up going to jail on Mother's Day 2010. I got clean and sober in jail and have stayed sober for 3 years now. I thought this would make God love me. I figured there must be a formula, three prayers a day? Two exclamations of "God Bless You!" a day or something else?

Then, on Dec 4, 2011 a tragedy took place that resulted in my mother's passing that Christmas Eve.

Again, my life was spinning out of control, but God had a plan. I went to the Community Resource Center and met Tom and Janis. I felt lost and desperate to not fall back into the addict lifestyle. I needed something to make sense in my life. I was struggling with a life time of devastation and pain. The volunteers embraced me and brought me into a circle of people that I felt the Lord was building for a purpose.

It was then that I met Chris and Kenny, both also homeless at the time; we forged a friendship that would change my life forever. I began to go to the winter homeless shelters and volunteer at the Community Resource Center. I even begin to believe "so this is how I can make God love me." Still not ready to get a clue what it was really about. Once again I began to struggle with severe depression and Post Traumatic Stress Disorder. I kept trying to will myself to be "OK".

Eight months later I was still trying to figure out what to do next. I was going to become homeless again and I didn't have any more ideas. I lost the will to fight any more. I finally just gave in and said to God, "Your will be done, Lord." That day I found myself walking up to the Hangtown Haven, the legal homeless camp on upper Broadway, scared of my own shadow, helpless, hopeless and totally lost in life.

I found a few friends there quickly! Now, I had a family which was actually the most stable, functional family I had ever had or imagined. Although imperfect, there is never a shortage of love, grace, support, compassion and encouragement. I found strength and began to grow and thrive.

A friend of mine in camp, James, asked me to join the other camp leaders to go to the Easter service at Green Valley Community Church. It sounded difficult and scary. Crowds can be very disturbing for me, but I was compelled to go. As soon as the music started I began to relax and I loved it. However, I was still trying to impress God. I still did not have the secret road map of how to gain God's love. I was sure I was getting God's attention but still wondered, "Is there a secret handshake?" Could that be it?"

One Sunday morning during the service at Green Valley, Pastor Ken let the secret slip. It was life-shattering for me, the answer to what I needed to do to get God to love me was...NOTHING.

There was nothing I could do make God love me. He already did, I just had to let him. What amazing news!

This also meant that there was nothing I could do to make God stop loving me. That day I cried my eyes out and felt the most unexplainable amazing peace of mind and soul. I would learn in the weeks to come that this was joy, real joy!"

Becky is one of the most intelligent, brilliant, natural leaders I know. I am blessed to know her and honored to baptize her this last summer. As Becky is getting back on her feet, she volunteers on Tuesdays and Thursdays at the church as the lead receptionist.

She keeps building her resume and learning new skills. I love when people call our church; the first person they talk to is a homeless person who connects them to the ministry they need help from. That makes me smile, but more importantly, I think it makes Jesus smile.

Every church must lead the way in caring for the homeless. I am not talking about occasionally doing something nice for people who do not have shelter.

I am **NOT** talking about dabbling in niceness with a yearly Thanksgiving or Christmas dinner. Though, that is a good start.

I am **NOT** talking about doing fly-bys where the homeless live.

I am **NOT** talking about waiting to see what the local government is going to do for those who are homeless and then complain that they are not doing enough.

I **AM** talking about fully engaging in discovering what the true needs are for those without shelter.

I **AM** talking about building long-term relationships with people, who for many diverse reasons, find themselves in difficult situations.

I **AM** talking about the church leading the way, by example, investing in people who God has mandated us to take care of - by providing food, clothing, shelter, life skill classes and more.

I **AM** talking about the church inviting the homeless into their church services, treating them like the brothers and sisters they are.

Focusing on those God asks us to care for allows our faith to grow and our priorities to change.

On one weekend, during the middle of winter, our clothing director told me that they needed men's shoes to give to men who spend time out in the elements with inadequate protection for their feet.

I announced during our weekend services that we needed men's shoes. Not the stinky, worn out shoes that we eventually get rid of. I told them we need nice shoes that will bring warmth and dignity for our guests.

As they left the services, men took off their shoes, their nice shoes (many pairs worth over $100) and left them in our lobby. They then walked to their cars in the pouring rain. We stocked up on over 200 pairs of shoes that day. One man told me that as he drove home in his wet socks it helped him have greater compassion for those who live out in cold, wet conditions. He told me it challenged him to simplify his life and to be more thankful for how blessed he was.

Steve and Kelly Stockwell and Tom and Janice Carney (dedicated volunteers) lead the way in how our church should respond to the plight of the homeless in our community. They put a face to the reality of homelessness and help us understand the complexity, challenges and even the prejudices and wrong stereotyping.

Last year during the winter season, several churches in our area created a rotating shelter where those who wanted shelter could stay at the designated church for the evening. Our church hosted our guests on Thursday and Friday nights. What a blessing it was for us. I think it was a blessing for them also. Thursday nights worked well because we have Celebrate Recovery on those nights. Those who struggle with hurts, habits and hang-ups could show up to the service, and then stay on campus and have a warm, dry place to sleep.

Friday nights worked well because our guests would wake up to our Saturday morning service we call "Common Ground", where they would receive a warm breakfast, groceries, clothing, prayer and love.

One man found himself homeless because of addictions. A self-proclaimed agnostic, he began to watch how these churches were opening their doors to him and praying for him, and he was blown away.

By spring, he became a follower of Jesus during Celebrate Recovery and is now making amends with those he had alienated and hurt. One of my concerns about having a central shelter in a community is that many times it gives the local church an "out."

People running shelters in other communities tell me that they have trouble getting churches involved. And if they do, they have a few people serve at the shelter, but they do not have the homeless go to their church.

I think the power of community, healing and hope will happen when the church begins to open its doors and services to the marginalized and forgotten.

Right now, we don't need to spend millions on a shelter when in every community; hundreds of thousands of square feet of shelter are already built. It is called the local church.

> **How many square feet in local churches sit empty 90% of the time? We don't need more shelters; we need to open the doors of the shelters we already have.**

It is time for the church to truly be the hands, feet and shelter that God has asked us to be. It is time to reintroduce the meaning of "sanctuary." We have enough square feet. We have enough shelter. We have enough resources.

But do we have enough faith and guts to invite these precious people into the places we worship?

It is time the church leads the way.
It will be messy.
It will be blessed.
It is where we meet Jesus.

"Then you will be known as a rebuilder of walls and a restorer of homes."
Isaiah 58:12 (NLT)

Measure of Effectiveness
#6. We have a growing sense of adventure, where people allow themselves to live on the edge of faith.

The Apostle Paul wrote that when we stand before God, with our unshakable, irremovable foundation being Grace, everything we built on that foundation that was not used to advance the Kingdom of God will be burned down (see 1 Corinthians 3:10-15).

Wasted time, neglected talents, selfish use of resources will go down in flames like kindling that helps start a campfire.

Paul's instruction is a warning but it is also a gift, reminding us that God has made us to live a high adrenaline, purpose filled, and legacy-leaving life.

Let's Do It Again Daddy!
When my son was seven years old, we went to Six Flags. One roller coaster went upside down. Your feet would hang free and you would free fall so it was quite a rush. Scary, but fun. At a young age, he was intimidated by the whole thing. When I tried to get him to ride it, he told me he was happy not to.

He was happy just walking around eating churros, drinking slurpees and hanging around the "throw-a-ring- around-a-bottle" game. Of course, nobody ever wins and if you do win, you have to lug a 30 pound Scooby Doo all around the park for the rest of the day. Churros and slurpees and stuffed animals are nice, but they're not why you go to Six Flags.

There is no adventure in them. Eventually, you get full, bloated and you run out of money.

The reason you go to Six Flags is for the thrill of the rides that put your stomach in your throat, speeds that knock your toupee off, and loops that sends blood rushing to your head. You scream, you laugh, you might even wet your pants, but at the end of the ride you know that you are fully alive!

I talked my son onto the ride even though he was still content hanging out with the churros, slurpees and stuffed animals. When he got on the ride, you could see fear in his face. During the ride, he screamed a little, he laughed a lot and I think he even wet his pants a little.

But when the ride came to an end, the thought of the mundane life of churros, slurpees and stuffed animals had left his head, and all he could say was, *"Daddy, let's do it again!"*

Jesus said in Luke 19:26 *"Risk your life and get more than you ever dreamed of. Play it safe and end up holding the bag."* (MSG)

God has an amazing adventure for all of us when we enter into his Kingdom. Adventures that will make us scream in terror, laugh with joy and maybe even wet our pants a little.

These are the adventures and life God created us for.

It is easy, when we get into the park (grace), to settle for safe, instant satisfying things...I mean, who doesn't like a hot churro and a cherry coke slurpee. But you have to eventually get on the scary rides, or you will miss out on the purpose of the Kingdom.

Nobody gets home from Six Flags and brags about how many churros and slurpees they ate and how much money they lost trying to win Scooby Doo. No, when you get home, you tell people all the scary rides you rode and how many times you rode them and how you can't wait to go back again and ride more!

As followers of Jesus, His grace gives us free access to the park, but once we are in, He asks us to get on the scary rides.

He asks us to not sit idly watching others ride, while you finish your fourth churro. He asks us to get on the ride and use our time, talents and treasures to feed the poor, shelter the homeless, relieve the oppressed, rescue the orphan, create spaces of sanctuary and safety, protect the widow, heal the sick, educate the next generation - all in the name of Jesus who came to heal the brokenhearted and set the captives free.

And it is true that on this ride, you may scream a little or laugh a lot and you might even wet your pants. However, I will guarantee you that when you get done with the ride, your first words out will be, *"Daddy, let's do it again!"*

Measure of Effectiveness
#7: We have a reputation for accepting rather than judging.

"You can safely assume you've created God in your own image when it turns out that God hates all the same people you do."
Anne Lamott, Author of Bird by Bird

Many of us have felt the emotional sting of being judged. A high school girl feels the rejection of not fitting with the "in crowd."

A divorced woman hears shaming comments from married friends evaluating her situation. She is looked upon as a failure.

A person of Arab descent notices people all around him staring as he sits in an airport waiting to visit family.

A single mom struggling to make ends meet, her car 15 years old, clothes out of fashion, notices that she seems invisible when she is in a crowd.

A man struggling with addiction has lost his family and messed up his career. He is afraid to talk to anyone about his issues for fear of being judged so continues in his pain.

We all know the sting of being judged. It is a sting that stays with us far after the judgment has been rendered. You may feel that sting right now.

Jesus said that he came to save the world and not to judge it. (See John 3:17)

Jesus knew the sting of being judged.

Jesus once spoke, *"Do not judge others, and you will not be judged. For you will be treated as you treat others. The standard you use in judging is the standard by which you will be judged."* Matthew 7:1-2 (NLT)

Have you ever judged someone because they were different than you? A couple of years ago I was working on a weekend message at a coffee shop. As I was working on a message which I am sure had to do with the love of God, I saw a young man walk through the doors. He was tatted up, wearing tight skinny jeans (ouch!) and a very tight tank top. He came strutting in like he owned the place. I do not have an issue with tattoos, but I did not like his body language. Plus, his jeans made me hurt. I instantly identified what this kid was all about.

He was a pompous, insecure, "life is all about me" kind of guy. You could just tell. That all came to me during the 30 seconds I looked at him standing in line to get a cup of coffee, or for him probably a Frappuccino.

I quickly got back to my message about God's love.

About 5 minutes later I noticed someone standing close to me. I tried to ignore this someone because I was putting together a message about the love of God. But it got a little awkward, so I looked up and standing there was this skinny-jeaned, Frappuccino loving, arrogant punk.

Great. Now what?

Before I could say anything he gently put his hand on my shoulder and said, *"You are the pastor at Green Valley aren't you?"* I didn't think it was a trick question, so I said, *"Yes, I am."* In my mind I was telling him to please hurry, I have to get this sermon on God's love done. He smiled and said, *"I want to thank you so much for all your church does. I have lived a pretty rough life, and I found Jesus and acceptance and recovery at your church."*

He then started getting emotional, and I started feeling like a complete idiot, and he finished with, *"And now I am starting to volunteer with high school students at the church helping them get on a good path, so they don't have to experience what I have experienced.*" He thanked me again and walked off with a smile on his face.

I tell you that story to show you what a spiritual giant I truly am.

You and I were made to be in the life-saving business, not in the judging business. The Apostle Paul once said, "Accept one another."
Romans 15:7 (NIV)

Those 3 words create a powerful sentence. To accept someone means to be "for them." It does not mean to approve of everything they do. It means to want what is best for them, no matter what they do.

Judging is the opposite of accepting.

A great example of Jesus accepting someone was when a woman who was caught in adultery by the religious "peeping Tom" leaders wanted to kill her with stones.

They said it was Moses' law and they needed to obey the law.

Jesus agreed and suggested that the one who had never sinned throw the first stone. No one could throw the stone (judge), because everyone had sinned.

Let me ask you a question: Have you ever held a stone in your hand? I think of myself as a pretty compassionate person, but I know I have.

Maybe that stone is...

A judgmental thought or comment about another race or culture. A self-righteous attitude towards those involved in a destructive sin. Gossiping or belittling someone who has a different political or theological view.

Fact: The energy you use holding onto the stone begins to drain the ability to love out of your heart.

It's hard to be in the life-saving business when your heart is empty of love. Mother Teresa once said, "*If you judge people, you have no time to love them."*

The scriptures say Jesus was a friend of sinners. They liked being around him and longed for his company. Meanwhile, legalists found him threatening and morally soft. The legalist separated "loving God" from "loving people." They thought it was possible to love God and throw stones.

> *"Prostitutes are in no danger of finding their present life so satisfactory that they cannot turn to God: the proud, the judgmental, the self-righteous, are in that danger."*
> **C.S. Lewis**

Jesus said, *"Let the one who has never sinned throw the first stone!"* John 8:7 (NLT)

What might a family, community, church or our world look like if nobody ever picked up a stone?

Do you have any stones you need to drop?

Big World, Small Minds

It's a big world with small minds
Distractions and riches make eyes blind
Egos clash, religions rage
God is love, just keep Him caged
Titles and treasures, I am willing to share it
I want to change the world, as long as I get the credit
Philosophies built on Fox News, CNN, Dr. Phil
I am afraid of the wrong things, naivety kills

Pray for my enemy, they were made in God's image
My prayers fall short, I divide who should be forgiven
It's easy to do good, but great is what we should
Better to fail at great, then to succeed at good

The shirt I wear, a kid made so far away
The rich get richer, while he barely gets paid
I should care about justice, I know it's wrong
But my appetite for things, my addictions are strong

I give God my all, I give God my best
As long as it fits my schedule, that is the test
I go to church to feel good, to be entertained
While in Niger, 1 of every 3 girls marries before fifteen

Girls exploited, objects of pleasure
Used as property, yet made as God's treasure
Seen as the least of these, yet so much potential
Educate, liberate and see the world more powerful

There is no longer Jew, Gentile or color
In the words of Mr. Hybels, "You have never looked into the eyes
of a person Jesus didn't die for."
We have the medicine, the resources to give
In the words of Mr. Hewson, "Where you live should not determine
whether you live."

Lose your life to find it, you are more blessed when giving
I'm holding on too tight, I've lost the point of living
My Father loves it when I invest and share it.
My culture loves it when I keep and spend it.

Life's mixed with blessings, struggles and pain
Make sure you laugh, cry and help those through the rain
The only thing certain, is that nothing is certain
Except for eternity, on the other side of the curtain

Today is a gift, tomorrow not guaranteed
Love overcomes evil, captives are freed
So what is required, Heaven will applaud
To act justly and to love mercy
and to walk humbly with your God.

MANDATE 7

A Culture of Celebration!

Mandate 7
A Culture of Celebration!

*"I think it pisses God off if you walk by the color purple
in a field somewhere and don't notice it."*
Alice Walker - Author, The Color Purple

*"Cultivate the habit of being grateful for every good thing that
comes to you, and to give thanks continuously. And because all
things have contributed to your advancement, you should include
all things in your gratitude."*
Ralph Waldo Emerson

*"Piglet noticed that even though he had a Very Small Heart,
it could hold a rather large amount of gratitude."*
A.A. Milne, Winnie-The-Pooh

Stories move people toward action. Churches and organizations trying to live out the Isaiah 58 mandate continually share and celebrate redemptive stories and miracles that happen all around us.

Successful leaders create a culture of celebration where those serving are energized by the continual telling of redemptive stories.

Some stories are personal to the church or particular ministry. Others are anchor stories to remind volunteers why living out the true fast of Isaiah 58 is the only way to live out their faith.

Churches living out Isaiah 58 have anchor stories to keep them focused and re-center them to the vision and value of the redemptive gospel.

Story #1: Living Compassion
I started sharing one such story 20 years ago when I started at GVCC, and I share it at least once a year ever since. It reminds us to stay sensitive to grace and compassionate towards those the world judges. Tony Campolo recalls a trip he and his wife took to Hawaii several years ago. Because of the time change, he couldn't fall asleep so he decided to take a walk down the streets of Honolulu during the middle of the night.

Around 3am, he walked into a little coffee shop for coffee and a doughnut. As he sat in the empty shop, four prostitutes walked in, talking loudly and ordering food after a night of work.

They seemed to know the guy working behind the counter, and as they chatted with him and each other, they teased one of the prostitutes named Agnes.

Apparently, her birthday was the next day and they were making jokes about her age, and wondering how long she could keep prostituting. Tony was sitting close and listening. Even though Agnes was laughing on the outside, he could tell by her voice and her tired face that the teasing hurt and her soul felt empty. They eventually got up and left but Tony got an idea.

He went to the gentlemen working behind the counter and asked if these ladies came in the shop every night about this time. The man said they usually came in around 3AM after turning tricks.

So Tony asked, "Would you help me throw a birthday party for Agnes the next morning? My wife and I will bring the decorations and the cake, if you will supply the dishes and silverware."

The man looked stunned but said he would go along with it. What else would he be doing at three in the morning? So Tony said, "It's a plan. See you here tomorrow, same time." Early the next morning, Tony and his wife set up the decorations and brought a cake that said, "Happy Birthday Agnes!" and they waited impatiently.

Promptly at 3am, the door opened and the ladies entered. Tony and his wife yell out, "Surprise!" and they sang Happy Birthday to Agnes. Agnes was stunned. She didn't know what to say. She began to cry. Then she laughed. Before they could cut the cake, Agnes asked if she could take the cake home and show her children. She never had a birthday cake before. Tony said, "Of course you can take it home." Agnes grabbed the cake and left the diner.

So here were Tony and his wife, sitting around with three prostitutes they did not know and the guy behind counter who seemed irritated by it all. Tony didn't know what to do and then it hit him. He announced to everyone in the room, "Let's pray for Agnes."

So Tony, his wife, three prostitutes and the guy behind the counter formed a little circle. Tony prayed that Agnes would have a great birthday and that she would experience God's grace and that she would understand how much God loved her.

When Tony said "Amen", the guy behind the counter belted out, "I didn't know this was some kind of religious gesture! If I would have known, I don't think I would have gotten involved. What kind of church do you go to anyway?" And Tony said the famous words that challenged my heart and our church to this day.

He said, "I go to a church that throws birthday parties for prostitutes at three in the morning."

The guy behind the counter then said, "No, you don't. Because if you did, I think I would go to that kind of church."

I think more people would go to church if there was more love, practical action and greater compassion. I pray that there will be a new movement of *"Churches throwing birthday parties for prostitutes at three in the morning."*

> *"Jesus lives in the forgotten. He has taken up residence in the ignored. He has made a mansion amidst the ill. If we want to see God we must go among the broken and beaten and there we will see them, we will see Him."*
> **Max Lucado - Author**

Challenges and bad news inundate us on a daily basis.

While being honest about these challenges and struggles, we must celebrate the victories and we must keep reminding people that while there are troubles all around us, we can take heart because Jesus has overcome the world.

Isaiah 58 leaders and churches are attractive because they are continually and strategically celebrating the amazing stories of God's faithfulness. A strategic successful leader incorporates the seven mandates into his or her celebrations, thus reinforcing their vision and values.

A successful leader will share about their broken heart. They will give a specific examples of what the comprehensive redemptive gospel looks like. Successful leaders brag on volunteers as a reminder of God's plan for everyone to be active with their time, talents and treasures. They celebrate the fruit of generosity, humility, selflessness and compassion for the poor so that during the celebration, the vision and values are embedding into the hearts of the people.

People need to know they are making a difference. It is important for leaders to continually remind their people that the gates of hell are not prevailing and that love is winning over evil.

At Green Valley, we see love winning all the time.

Locally, we see the homeless finding jobs and shelter and faith. We see addicts overcoming through the same power that raised Christ from the dead. We see lonely seniors experiencing new found dignity and love. We see people who were far from God finding life-changing Grace. We see people who were living selfish lives giving their lives over to serving those who God calls us to serve.

We also see the local government, school districts and businesses looking to Green Valley for help. They know the Church as a deeply committed organization that wants to see their community grow strong and healthy, with no strings attached. It's called unconditional love.

Globally, at Green Valley, we see 1500 children being sponsored through Compassion International. We see a home being built and recovery found at the Courage Home in New Delhi, India which rescues and rehabilitates young girls from the horrors of sex-trafficking. We see homes being built, orphans being loved, hungry children being fed and brilliant minds being educated in the garbage dumps of Tijuana, Mexico. We see our American congregation becoming aware of the global realities of poverty and it has caused a transformational change of their lifestyle.

Story #2: My Journey to Africa, A Rock Star and The Power of a Child
My journey to Africa started with a rock star from Ireland telling me the church had missed the point. While the Christian world was arguing over who was going to heaven and who was going to hell, Paul Hewson (a.k.a. Bono) was reminding us that thousands of children in Africa were dying every day from preventable diseases such as malaria, cholera, typhoid fever, dysentery and even HIV.

Jesus came to preach "Good News" to the poor, and yet His bride, the Church, by its apathy, was telling the poor that the "Good News" was not for them.

Mr. Hewson reminded us that in the final judgment, Jesus would not ask us about how solid our doctrine was, how pure our thoughts were or what side of the political aisle we were on. No, He would ask us how we treated the hungry, the homeless, the naked, the imprisoned, the poor. That was it.

No caveats. Pretty clear and simple. I was sitting there wondering how we had complicated it and missed the mark so badly.

But how was I supposed to help Africa? Where could I start? The ONE campaign was one way, and it was a good way, but I needed something more long term, more hands on. I needed something I could get our whole church behind.

I didn't want to reinvent the wheel, but I also wanted to make sure we got involved with an organization that was having a huge impact in defeating poverty and had opportunities for anyone and everyone to be involved.

Compassion International fit this template. It is a holistic organization that helps the poorest of the poor with education, healthcare, social skills, community, an introduction to the local church and most of all, a relationship with Jesus. And best of all, through the child sponsorship program, anyone and everyone could participate. From students to senior citizens, everyone could sponsor a child and save a life. Actually, they would not only save a life, but propel a life toward being the leader of change in his or her community.

We needed to decide where in Africa we wanted to partner with Compassion.

Green Valley has a philosophy to go to the most difficult places, so I called Compassion and asked them, "What African country would you recommend our church get involved with?" The answer was, "We are just starting in a new country called Burkina Faso, and we would love if your church would focus in on this region. It is such a poor country and people tend to focus on east Africa or South Africa, but this is a forgotten region."

My response was, *"Burkina Fa...what?"* I had never heard of it before and had to look at a map. Burkina Faso didn't even sound like an African name. Rwanda, Uganda, Kenya, Ethiopia were all familiar African names, but Burkina Faso?

The leaders at Compassion International said it was an extremely poor country, wide open to the hope of child advocacy. We agreed to pray about it before our big Compassion sponsorship weekend.

Just after that conversation, a team from my church flew to Washington D.C. to work with some inner city ministries. We decided to visit the Burkina Faso embassy to learn about the country. Driving down Massachusetts Ave in the northwest quadrant of Washington D.C. is impressive. The architectural brilliance of the Japanese and British Embassies helped create a harsh reality of how poor the country Burkina Faso was. We drove up the street, to a narrow two-story row house made of brick, tucked away, only recognizable by the small Burkina Faso flag waving above the weathered front door.

As we entered the building, the lobby had a few misplaced pictures on the wall. There was a waiting room with faded wood floors next to the lobby filled with mismatched chairs and furniture. We went upstairs to meet with a representative and they ushered us into a boardroom that was simple but functional. The people were kind and very surprised to have guests. We told them that we were getting ready to invest in hundreds of children through Compassion International's sponsorship program in their country. We wanted to know the main things we should be praying for.

The gentlemen and his assistant seemed startled by the request. They told us to pray for enough rain—not too much, not too little—just enough so that their crops would be plentiful this year. They told us to pray for those infected by malaria and other diseases, and to pray for the families that were living under the weight of extreme poverty.

We prayed together, and as we were saying our goodbyes, a gentleman pulled me aside and said, *"Thank you so much for coming here. We have never had anyone come into the embassy to pray for us. I am a Christian, and I am so excited about your work with Compassion. I will be praying for you and your church that you will be blessed by blessing my country."* I will never forget that kind, hopeful smile.

Later that day, at a restaurant in China town, the busboy at our table said, *"Thank you for coming, have a nice day,"* with a very thick African accent. We walked out the door, but something prompted me to go back in and ask the young man where he was from. I walked back in and asked the young man about his home country and he said, *"I am from Burkina Faso."*

Tears filled my eyes as I smiled, shook his hand and told him *"God bless you and your country."* He smiled and said very sweetly, *"Thank you. My country is beautiful and very much in need of God's blessings."*

I walked out on to the busy streets of D.C. in amazement of how God works. I had never heard of Burkina Faso a few weeks before and I had certainly never met anyone from there. But within one day, I got to pray in its embassy and meet someone from there "randomly" at a restaurant.

God certainly has a way of showing us what we should be involved with.

A month later, families from our church sponsored about 400 children from Burkina Faso and Bono's words had taken effect. Today, we sponsor about 600 children from Burkina Faso and over 1500 children world-wide.

Since then, I have been to Burkina Faso twice to see many of the Compassion projects and churches in the capital town of Ouagadougou. I was able to spend time with my family's sponsored children from Burkina Faso - Lionel, Issouf and Larissa. They are more beautiful than you can imagine.

Words seem to fall short when trying to describe the impact Compassion International is making around the world for the poor. I knew that this company helped children, but never could I imagine the lengths and depth to which it reaches.

We saw children going to school, being tutored, going to extra-curricular projects and receiving both simple and life- saving health care. I sat in a dark, stifling hot hut of a mother and sponsored child. Both were HIV-positive and fully alive because of the HIV antiviral drugs provided by Compassion. We saw micro-financing for families in the program that allowed greater profits and business education for sustainability.

We saw clean water brought into projects and villages along with education about water and the importance of washing hands before meals. We saw thousands of children introduced to the love, grace, hope and redemption of Jesus.

Compassion International is walking the talk, investing and creating a powerful future for the next generations.

One of the most impacting days was when a few of us walked into a very poor Muslim village on the outskirts of Ouagadougou, where several Muslim families had children sponsored by Compassion. We bought large bags of rice, cooking oil and soap for many of the families.

They proudly showed us their clay huts with tin roofs. We saw one room homes that housed simple open fire kitchens while sleeping eight. Even with a large language barrier, we could see their gratitude and excitement to show off their dwelling places.

Just before we left, a mother stopped me and asked if we could pray for her son because he was sick. Her son looked like he possibly had malaria. He was lying under a shade tree in the 100 degree weather, with a blanket covering him, shivering from the effects of a life-threatening mosquito bite. We knelt down and with deep respect prayed for the young man. We prayed for the village, for the mothers and for the families. When we were done praying and opened our eyes, about 20 moms had lined up with their babies and children for us to pray for them. Muslim mothers who knew we were Christians, asking us to pray for their children. Chills went down my spine and I knew this was one of those divine moments that all you can do is smile, be obedient and take it all in.

All of these events were not accidents, but God's divine plan. We just must listen closely to his voice and to his clues.

I return to Africa often. Seeing Burkina Faso experiencing the blessings of Compassion first hand, we are now working on child advocacy and strengthening the Church in the neighbor country of Niger. Compassion will eventually enter there also.

Africa is a beautiful continent with smart, lovely people who do not need our pity, just an opportunity. With education, health care, and spiritual development these children can change the face of Africa. Thank you Mr.

Hewson (a.k.a. Bono) for kick-starting God's miracle work in West Africa. Thank you for waking the Church up. If you have never sponsored a child through Compassion, I would like to encourage you to do so today: **www.compassion.com**

WRAP UP

What Will be Said?

Wrap Up
What Will be Said?

WHAT WILL BE SAID OF OUR GENERATION?
A generation blinded by wealth where poverty cannot be seen.
A generation who talks about feeding the hungry while paying
for Weight Watchers because they can't stop eating.
A generation that believes in sheltering the homeless,
as long as they're not near their own over-bloated homes.
A generation that worries about their growing status and
expanding pleasures while children are worried
about empty bellies and fragile futures.

WHAT WILL BE SAID OF OUR GENERATION?
A generation that is more globally aware than any other generation
yet is obsessed with celebrity reality shows and stock market results.
A generation that is technologically brilliant yet socially stunted.
A generation that knows things ARE getting better
but is afraid to finish the job.
A generation that is torn between self-indulgence
and self-righteousness.

WHAT WILL BE SAID OF OUR GENERATION?
There is enough food for everyone.
Churches have more roofs than there are homeless.
Most diseases that kill are preventable.
The lack of education is fixable.

WHAT WILL BE SAID OF OUR GENERATION?
We prayed for the poor while building bigger barns.
We preached for justice while closing our eyes.
We fought sex trafficking while watching pornography.
We judged the homosexual while worshipping our idols.

WHAT WILL BE SAID OF OUR GENERATION?
We ignored building God's Kingdom while building our own.
We gossiped of our brothers and sisters while
singing songs to our Creator.
We multi-tasked and networked while sitting alone.
We opened our mouths to poverty while
closing our wallets to solution.

BUT WHAT COULD BE SAID OF OUR GENERATION?

We tithed our first 10%, creating a mass of wealth that
stunned the world and ended extreme poverty.
We adopted the orphan, ending the foster system as we know it.
We supported organizations like International Justice Mission,
declaring that the end of slavery would happen on our watch.
We sponsored children around the world ensuring them an education,
antiviral HIV drugs and an introduction to faith.

WHAT SHOULD BE SAID OF OUR GENERATION?

We decided that the gates of hell would not prevail
and good would win over evil.
We decided that the most important part of a church service
is what happens once we leave the parking lot.
We decided that it doesn't profit to gain
the whole world but lose our soul.
We decided that God is close to broken hearts
and crushed spirits.

WHAT DO I HOPE WILL BE SAID OF OUR GENERATION?

We shunned consumerism and found joy in minimalism.
We ignored the American dream and pursued God's pleasure.
We simplified our lives so that others could simply live.
We preached always and occasionally spoke words.

*"God is in the slums, in the cardboard boxes where the poor play house.
God is in the silence of a mother who has infected her child with a virus
that will end both their lives. God is in the cries heard under the rubble
of war. God is in the debris of wasted opportunity and lives,
and God is with us if we are with them."*
Bono

About The Author

Ken Burkey was the Senior Pastor at Green Valley Community Church in Placerville, California for 24 years and tries his best to position his life to be an advocate to the poor - speaking, writing and traveling to inspire people towards justice and grace. He is now using his new platform as the Executive Director of Live58 to empower other churches and communities to live out the Isaiah 58 fast.

He is the husband of Penny and the father of Kenny and Larissa. His life has been motivated by Paul Hewson (a.k.a. Bono) and he is a desperate follower of Jesus of Nazareth. His favorite book is Oh, the Places You'll Go! by Dr. Seuss and his favorite quote is "Preach the Gospel at all times, and when necessary, use words" by St. Francis of Assisi.

Acknowledgements:

First of all, I want to thank my wife Penny and my children, Kenny and Larissa, who are the best examples of bringing hope to the most vulnerable. Thank you for keeping me focused on what breaks the heart of God. They inspire me and make me a much better person. I am so blessed and it's not because I deserve it. It's called GRACE.

I am also grateful for the immeasurable support and example of my church family and volunteers who not only share this journey with me but continue to amaze me in their creativity and compassion to persistently live out the principles outlined in Isaiah 58.

And, for the dedicated pastors and leaders who met to discuss the needs of churches desiring to live out Isaiah 58. Together, we defined the mandates outlined in this book: Dr. Jerry Edmonson, Dr. Scott Todd, Deb Brown, Lori Hahn, Charley Scandlyn, Mark Swarner, Ed Rowell, Montie Ralstin, Greg Johnson, Chad Erlenborn, Matt Petersen, Rob Harvey, Jonathan Bell, Steve Grey, Hope Forti, and Angelina Dieleman - I will never forget how God orchestrated that November meeting in Northern California.

Made in the USA
San Bernardino, CA
20 September 2016